NOTES ON RESISTANCE

NOTES ON RESISTANCE

NOAM CHOMSKY AND DAVID BARSAMIAN

Haymarket Books
Chicago, Illinois

Published in 2022 by
Haymarket Books
P.O. Box 180165
Chicago, IL 60618
773-583-7884
www.haymarketbooks.org
info@haymarketbooks.org

ISBN: 978-1-64259-698-4

Distributed to the trade in the US through Consortium Book Sales
and Distribution (www.cbsd.com) and internationally through Ingram
Publisher Services International
(www.ingramcontent.com).

This book was published with the generous support of Lannan Foundation and Wallace Action Fund.

Special discounts are available for bulk purchases by organizations
and institutions. Please email info@haymarketbooks.org for more
information.

Cover design by Steve Leard.

Printed in Canada by union labor.

Library of Congress Cataloging-in-Publication data is available.

10 9 8 7 6 5 4 3 2 1

CONTENTS

THE DECISION THAT HAS TO BE MADE

Let's talk about Iran, in particular, in post-1945 US foreign policy. Washington laid out its "Grand Area" strategy, and Iran takes on enormous significance because of its oil wealth.

Oil wealth and strategic position. It was taken for granted in the Grand Area strategy planning that the United States would dominate the Middle East, what Eisenhower called the strategically most important part of the world, a material prize without any analogue.

The basic idea of the early stage of the Grand Strategy and the early stages of the war was that the United States would take over what they called the Grand Area, of course, the Western Hemisphere, also the former British Empire and the Far East. They assumed at that time that Germany would probably win the war, so there would be two major powers, one German-based with a lot of Eurasia, and the United States with this Grand Area. By the time it was clear that the Russians would defeat Germany, after Stalingrad and then the great tank battle in Kursk, the planning was modified, and the idea became that the Grand Area would include as much of Eurasia as possible, of course maintaining control of Middle East oil resources.

There was a conflict over Iran right at the end of the Second World War. The Russians supported a separatist movement in the north. The British wanted to maintain control. The Russians were essentially expelled. Iran was a client state under British control. There was, however, a nationalist movement, and the Iranian leader, Mohammad Mossadegh, led a movement to try to nationalize Iranian oil.

The British, obviously, didn't want that. They tried to stop this development, but they were in their postwar straits and were unable to do it. They called in the United States, which basically took the prime role in implementing a military coup that deposed the parliamentary regime and installed the Shah, who was a loyal client.

Iran remained one of the pillars of control of the Middle East as long as the Shah remained in power. The Shah had very close relations with Israel, the second pillar of control. The ties were not formal because theoretically the Islamic states were supposed to be opposed to Israeli occupation, but relations were extremely close. They were revealed in detail after the Shah fell. The third pillar of US control was Saudi Arabia, so there was kind of a tacit alliance between Iran and Israel and, even more tacit, Israel and Saudi Arabia, under US aegis.

In 1979, the Shah was overthrown. The United States at first considered trying to implement a military coup that would restore the Shah's regime. That didn't work. Then came the hostage crisis. Shortly after, Iraq, under Saddam Hussein, invaded Iran. The United States strongly supported the Iraqi invasion, finally even pretty much intervening directly to protect Iraqi shipping in the Gulf. In 1988, a US missile cruiser shot down a civilian Iranian airliner, killing 290 people in commercial airspace. Finally, the US intervention pretty much convinced the Iranians, if not to capitulate, then to accept an arrangement for far less than they hoped after the Iraqi aggression. It was a murderous war. Saddam used chemical weapons. The US pretended not to know about it—and, in fact, tried to blame Iran for it. But there was finally a peace agreement.

The US at once turned to sanctions against Iran and severe threats. This was now the first President Bush. His administration also invited Iraqi nuclear engineers to the United States for advanced training in nuclear weapons production, which, of course, was a serious threat to Iran.

It's kind of ironic that when Iran was a loyal client state under the Shah in the 1970s, the Shah and other high officials made it very clear that they were working to develop nuclear weapons. At that time, Henry Kissinger, Donald Rumsfeld, and Dick Cheney were pressuring US universities, primarily MIT—there was a big flap on campus about this—to bring Iranian nuclear engineers to the United States for training, though, of course, they knew they were developing nuclear weapons. Actually, Kissinger was asked later why he changed his attitude toward Iranian nuclear weapons development in later years when, of course, it became a big issue, and he said, very simply, they were an ally then.

The sanctions against Iran got harsher, more intense. There were negotiations about dealing with the Iranian nuclear programs. According to US intelligence, there was no evidence that Iran had nuclear weapons programs after 2003, but probably they were developing what's called a nuclear capability, which many countries have—that is, the capacity to produce nuclear weapons if the occasion arises. As Iran was rapidly increasing its capacities, with more centrifuges and so on, President Obama finally agreed to the joint agreement, the Iran nuclear deal, as it's informally called, in 2015.

Since then, according to US intelligence, Iran has completely lived up to the agreement. There is no indication of any Iranian violation. The Trump administration pulled out of the deal and has now sharply escalated the sanctions against Iran. Now there is a new pretext. It's not nuclear weapons; it's that Iran is "meddling" in the region.

Unlike the United States.

Or every other country. In fact, what they're saying is Iran is attempting to extend its influence in the region. It has to become what Secretary of State Mike Pompeo called a "normal country," like us, Israel, and others, and never try to expand its influence.[1] Essentially, it's saying, just capitulate. Pompeo particularly has said that US sanctions are designed to reduce Iranian oil exports to zero. The United States has extraterritorial influence: it forces other countries to accept US sanctions under threat that they will be excluded from the US market and, in particular, from financial markets, which are dominated by the United States. So the United States, as the world's leading rogue state, enforces its own unilateral decisions on others, thanks to its power. John Bolton, of course, said he just wants to "bomb Iran."[2]

My speculation is that a lot of the fist waving at the moment is probably for two reasons. The first is to try to keep Iran off balance and intimidated, and also intimidate others so that they don't try to interfere with US sanctions. The second, I think, is largely domestic. If the Trump strategists are thinking clearly—and I assume they are—the best way to approach the 2020 election is to concoct major threats all over: immigrants from Central America coming here to commit genocide against white Americans, Iran about to conquer the world, China doing this and that. But we will be saved by our bold leader with the orange hair, the one person capable of defending us from all of these terrible threats, not like these women who won't know how to do anything or Sleepy Joe or Crazy Bernie. That's the best way to move into an election. That means maintaining tensions but not intending actually to go to war.

Unfortunately, it's bad enough in itself. We have absolutely zero right to impose any sanctions on Iran. None. It's taken for granted in all discussion that somehow this is legitimate. There is absolutely no basis for that. But also, tensions can easily blow up. Anything could happen. An American ship in the Gulf could hit a mine, let's say, and some commander would say, "Okay, let's retaliate against an Iranian installation," and then an Iranian ship could shoot a missile. Pretty soon, you're off and running. So, it could blow up.

Meanwhile, there are horrible effects all over the place. The worst is in Yemen, where our client, Saudi Arabia, with strong US support—arms, intelligence—along with its brutal United Arab Emirates ally, is creating what the United Nations (UN) has described as "the worst humanitarian crisis in the world."[3] It's pretty clear. It's not really controversial what's happening.

If there is a confrontation with Iran, the first victim will be Lebanon. As soon as there's any threat of war, Israel will certainly be unwilling to face the danger of Hezbollah missiles, which are probably scattered all around Lebanon by now. So, it's very likely that the first step prior to direct conflict with Iran would be essentially to wipe out Lebanon, or something like it.

And those missiles in Lebanon are from Iran.

They come from Iran, yes.

So what is Iran's strategy in the region? You hear this term, the "Shi'a arc," referring to the Shi'a populations in Iraq, Bahrain, Lebanon, and Syria.

The Shi'a arc is a Jordanian concoction. Of course, Iran, like every other power, is trying to extend its influence. It's doing it, typically, in the Shi'a areas, naturally. It's a Shi'ite state. In Lebanon, we don't have detailed records because they can't take a census—it would break down the fragile relationship that exists there in the sectarian system—but it's pretty clear that the Shi'ite population is the largest of the sectarian groups.

The Shi'ite population have a political representative, Hezbollah, which is in the parliament. Hezbollah developed as a guerilla force. Israel was occupying southern Lebanon after its 1982 invasion. This was in violation of UN orders, but they pretty much stayed there, in part through a proxy army. Hezbollah finally drove Israel out. That turned them into a "terrorist force." You're not allowed to drive out the invading army of a client state, obviously.

Since then, Hezbollah has served Iranian interests. It sent fighters to Syria, which are a large part of the support for the Bashar al-Assad government. Technically, that's quite legal. That was the recognized government. It's a rotten government, so you can, on moral grounds, say you shouldn't do it, but you can't say on legal grounds you shouldn't.

The United States was openly trying to overthrow the government. It's not secret. Finally, it became clear that the Assad government would control Syria. There are a few pockets still left unresolved, the Kurdish areas and others, but it's pretty much won the war, which means that Russia and Iran have the dominant role in Syria.

In Iraq, there is a Shi'ite majority, and the US invasion of Iraq pretty much handed the country over to Iran. It had been under a Sunni dictatorship, but, of course, with the Sunni dictatorship destroyed, the Shi'a population gained a substantial role. So, for example, when ISIS came pretty close to conquering Iraq, it was the Shi'ite militias that drove them back, with Iranian support. The United States participated, but secondarily. Now they have a strong role in the government. In the United States, this is considered more "Iranian meddling," but I think Iran's strategy is pretty straightforward. It's to expand their influence in the region.

As far as their military posture is concerned, I don't see any reason to question the analysis of US intelligence agencies. It seems pretty accurate. In their presentations to Congress, they point out that Iran has very low military expenditures by the standards of the region, much less than the other countries—it's dwarfed by the UAE and Saudi Arabia, and of course Israel—and its military doctrine is essentially defensive, designed to deter an invasion long enough for diplomatic efforts to be initiated. According to US intelligence, if they have a nuclear weapons program—which we have no reason to believe they do, but if they do—it would be part of their deterrent strategy.

That's the real Iranian threat: it has a deterrent strategy. For the states that want to be free to rampage in the region, deterrence is an existential threat. You don't want to be deterred. You want to be able to do what you like. That's primarily the United States and Israel. Both want to be free to act forcefully in the region without any deterrent. So, to be accurate, that's the real Iranian threat. It's what the State Department calls "successful defiance." That's the term the State Department used to explain back in the early 1960s why we cannot tolerate the Fidel Castro regime in Cuba, because of its "successful defiance" of the United States. That's absolutely intolerable if you intend to be able to rule the world, by force, if necessary.

And it seems a component of that is the threat of a good example.

There's also that, but I don't think that's true in the case of Iran. It's a miserable government. The Iran government is a threat to its own people. I think that's fair enough to say. And it's not a real model for anyone.

Cuba was quite different. In fact, if you look back at the internal documents that have been declassified, there was great concern in the early 1960s that, as Arthur Schlesinger, Kennedy's close adviser, particularly on Latin American affairs, said, the problem with Cuba is "the spread of the Castro idea of taking matters into one's own hands," which has great appeal to others in the region who are suffering from the same circumstances as Cuba under the US-backed regime of Fulgencio Batista.[4]

That's dangerous. The idea that people have the right to take things into their own hands and separate themselves from US domination is not acceptable. That's successful defiance.

Another theme that plays out post-1945 is Washington's resistance to independent nationalism.

Yes. But that's automatic for a hegemonic power. The same is true of Britain when it was running most of the world. The same with France and its domains. You don't want independent nationalism. In fact, it's often made quite explicit. Right after the Second World War, when the United States was beginning to try to organize the postwar world, the first concern was to make sure that the Western Hemisphere was totally under control.

In February 1945, the United States called a hemispheric conference in Chapultepec, Mexico. The main theme of the conference was precisely what you described, to end any kind of "economic nationalism." That was the phrase that was used. The State Department internally warned that Latin American countries are infected by the idea of the "new nationalism," which meant that the people of the country should be the first beneficiaries of the country's resources. Obviously, that's totally intolerable. The first beneficiaries have to be US investors. So, the philosophy of the new nationalism has to be crushed. And the Chapultepec Conference, in fact, made it explicit that economic nationalism would not be tolerated.

Incidentally, there is, as always, one unmentioned exception to the rules. The United States is permitted to follow policies of economic nationalism. In fact, the United States was pouring government resources massively into development of what became the high-tech economy of the future: computers, the internet, and so on. That's the usual exception. But for the others, they can't succumb to this idea that the first beneficiaries of a country's resources should be the people of that country. That's intolerable. This is framed in all sorts of nice rhetoric about free markets and so on and so forth, but the meaning is quite explicit.

You've often quoted George Kennan, the well-respected, venerated State Department official. In his famous 1948 memo, he observed, "[We] have about 50 percent of the world's wealth but only 6.3 percent of its population . . . . Our real task in the coming period is to devise a pattern of relationships which will permit us to maintain this position of disparity."[5] That was 1948. I was

interested to discover that two years later he made a statement about Latin America to the effect, "The protection of our raw materials" in the rest of the world, particularly in Latin America, would trump concern over what he called "police repression."[6]

He said police repression may be necessary to maintain control over "our resources." Remember that he was at the dovish extreme of the policy spectrum; in fact, so much so that he was replaced by a hard-liner, Paul Nitze. He was considered too soft for this tough world.

His estimate of the United States having 50 percent of the world's resources is probably exaggerated now that more careful work has been done. The statistics aren't great for that period, but it was probably less than that. However, it may be true today in a different sense. In the contemporary period of globalization and global supply chains, national accounts, meaning the country's share of global gross domestic product, is much less relevant than it used to be. A much more relevant measure of a country's power is the wealth controlled by domestically based multinational cor-porations. There what you find is that US corporations own about 50 percent of world wealth.

Now there are good statistics. There are studies of this by a very good political economist, Sean Kenji Starrs, who has several arti-cles and a new book coming out on it with extensive details.[7] As he points out, this is a degree of control of the international economy that has absolutely no parallel or counterpart in history, in fact.

It will be interesting to see what the impact of Trump's wreck-ing ball is on all of this, which is breaking the system of global supply chains that have been carefully developed over the years.

Getting back to Iran, you mentioned in our book *Global Dis-contents* that "any concern about Iranian weapons of mass de-struction (WMDs) could be alleviated by the simple means of heeding Iran's call to establish a WMD-free zone in the Middle East."[8] This is almost on the level of samizdat. It's barely known or reported on.

It's not a secret. And it's not just Iran's call. This proposal for a nuclear weapons–free zone in the Middle East—and extended to WMD-free zone—actually comes from the Arab states. Egypt and others initiated that back in the early 1990s. They called for a nuclear weapons–free zone in the Middle East.

There are such zones that have been established in several parts of the world. It's interesting to look at them. They aren't fully operative, because the United States has not accepted them, but they're theoretically there. One for the Middle East would be extremely important.

The Arab states pushed for a nuclear weapons–free zone for a long time. The nonaligned countries, the G-77—which has grown by now to about 130 countries—called strongly for it. Iran, as the spokesperson for the G-77, strongly pushed for it. Europe pretty much supports it. Probably not England, but others. In fact, there is almost total global support for this, adding to it an inspection regime of a kind that already exists in Iran. That would essentially eliminate any concern over, not only nuclear weapons but weapons of mass destruction.

There's only one problem: the United States won't allow it. This comes up regularly at the regular reviews of the Non-Proliferation Treaty, most recently in 2015. Obama blocked it. And everybody knows exactly why. Nobody will say, of course. But if you look at the arms control journals or professional journals, they're quite open about it, because it's obvious. If there were such an agreement, Israel's nuclear weapons would come under international inspection. The United States would be compelled to formally acknowledge that Israel has nuclear weapons. Of course, Washington knows that it does—everybody does—but you're not allowed to formally acknowledge it.

For a good reason. If you formally acknowledge Israel's nuclear weapons, US aid to Israel has to terminate under US law. Of course, you can find ways around it. You can always violate your own laws. But that does become a problem. It would mean that

Israel's weapons—not just nuclear, but also biological and chemical—would have to be inspected. That's intolerable, so we can't allow that. Therefore, we can't move toward a WMD-free zone, which would end the problem.

There is another thing that you can only read in samizdat. The United States has a special commitment to this policy, along with Britain. The reason is that when the United States and Britain, its British poodle, were planning the invasion of Iraq, they sought desperately to find some legal cover so it wouldn't just look like direct aggression. They appealed to a 1991 UN Security Council resolution that called on Saddam Hussein to end Iraq's nuclear weapons programs, which in fact he had done. But the pretext was he hadn't, so he had violated the resolution—and that was supposed to give some legitimacy to the invasion.

If you bother reading the UN resolution, when you get down to article 14, it commits the signers, including the United States and Britain, to work for a nuclear weapons–free zone in the Middle East.[9] So the United States and Britain have a unique responsibility to do this. Try to find any discussion of this fact. And, of course, it could resolve whatever problem one thinks there is. In fact, according to US intelligence, there is essentially none.

The real problem is pretty much what US intelligence describes, the Iranian posture of deterrence. That is a real danger and is constantly regarded as an existential threat to Israel and the United States, which cannot tolerate deterrence.

There are big paydays for a militaristic foreign policy. For example, Lee Fang, writing in the Intercept, reports, "Large arms manufacturers," like Lockheed Martin and Raytheon, have "told investors that escalating conflict with Iran could be good for business."[10]

Of course it is. That's a factor. I don't think it's the major factor, but it certainly is a factor. It's "good for the economy" if you can produce material goods that you can sell to other countries. The United States is preeminent in military force. That's its real comparative advantage—military force. Other countries can produce computers and televisions, but the United States is the largest arms exporter. Its military budget overwhelms anything in the rest of the world. In fact, it's almost as large as the rest of the world's combined, much larger than other countries'.

The increase in the military budget under Trump—the increase—is greater than the entire Russian military budget.[11] China is way behind. And, of course, the United States is way more technologically advanced in military hardware.

So, that's the US comparative advantage. You would naturally want to pursue it. But I think the major thing is just ensuring that the world remains pretty much under control.

Do you ever make the connection between the external violence of the US state and what is happening internally?

The US is a very strange country. From the point of view of its infrastructure, the United States often looks like a third world country. If you take a plane from Europe and land at Kennedy airport, and try to get into New York, it's like being somewhere in the third world. Not for everybody, of course. There are people who can say, "I'll go in my helicopter."

Drive around any US city. They're falling apart. The American Society of Civil Engineers gives the United States regularly a D, the lowest ranking, in infrastructure.

This is the richest country in world history. It has enormous resources. It has advantages that are just incomparable in agricultural and mineral resources, with huge, homogenous territory. You can fly three thousand miles and think you're in the same place where you started. There is nothing like that anywhere in the world.

In fact, there are successes, like a good deal of the high-tech economy, substantially government based but real. On the other hand, it's the only country in the developed world in which mortality is actually increasing. That's just unknown in developed societies.

In the last several years, life expectancy has declined in the United States. There is work by two economists, Anne Case and Angus Deaton, who have carefully studied the mortality figures.[12] It turns out that in the cohort roughly of 25 to 50, the working-age cohort of whites, the white working class, there is an increase in deaths, what they call "deaths of despair"—suicide, opioid overdoses, and so on. This is estimated at about 150,000 deaths a year. It's not trivial. The reason, presumably, it's generally assumed, is the economic stagnation since the early 1980s, when neoliberal programs began to be instituted.

That has led to a small slowdown in growth. Growth is not what it was before. There is growth, but it's very highly concentrated. Wealth has become extremely highly concentrated. Right now, according to the latest figures, 0.1 percent of the population holds 20 percent of the country's wealth. The top 1 percent holds roughly 40 percent. Half the population has negative net worth, meaning debts outweigh assets.[13] There has been stagnation for much of the workforce over the whole neoliberal period. That's the group that we're talking about.

Naturally, this leads to anger, resentment, desperation. Similar things are happening in Europe under austerity programs. That's the background for what's misleadingly called populism. But in the United States, it's quite striking. The "deaths of despair" phenomenon seems to be a specific US characteristic, not matched in other countries.

Remember, there is no country in the world that has anything like the advantages of the United States in wealth, power, and resources. It's a shocking commentary.

You read constantly that the unemployment rate has reached a wonderful level, barely 3 percent unemployed. But that's pretty misleading. When you use Labor Department statistics, it turns out that the actual unemployment rate is more than 7 percent. When you take into account the large number of people who have just dropped out of the workforce, labor force participation is considerably below what it was about twenty to thirty years ago. There are good studies of this by economists. You have roughly a 7.5 percent unemployment rate and stagnation of real wages, which have barely moved. Since the year 2000, there has been a steady decline in real median family wealth. As I said, for about half the population it's now negative.

There are many kinds of third world characteristics that are extremely striking in the richest, most powerful country in the world, with incomparable advantages.

In terms of guns, the United States is an outlier. We have 4 percent of the world's population and 40 percent of the guns.

There is an interesting history to that, very well studied. There's a recent book by Pamela Haag called *The Gunning of America: Business and the Making of American Gun Culture.*[14] It's a very interesting analysis. What she shows is that gun manufacturers didn't really have much of a market after the Civil War. The US government market had declined, of course, and foreign governments weren't much of a market.

In the late nineteenth century, the United States was an agricultural society. Farmers had guns, but they were like tools, nothing special. You had a nice old-fashioned gun. It was enough to chase away wolves. They didn't want the fancy guns that gun manufacturers were producing.

So, an enormous campaign was carried out to try to create a gun culture. This was the first huge advertising campaign, kind of a model for others later. They invented the Wild West, which never existed, with the bold sheriff drawing the pistol faster than anyone else and all this nonsense that you see in cowboy movies. It was all concocted. Cowboys were sort of the dregs of society, people who couldn't get a job anywhere else. You hired them to push some cows around or something. But this image of the Wild West and the great heroes was developed. Along with it came the ads, saying that if your son doesn't have a Winchester rifle, he's not a real man. If your daughter doesn't have a little pink pistol, she'll never be happy.

It was a tremendous success. I suppose it was a model for when the tobacco companies developed the "Marlboro Man" and all that kind of business. This was the late nineteenth, early twentieth century, the period in which a huge public relations industry was beginning to develop. It was brilliantly discussed by Thorstein Veblen, the great political economist, who pointed out that in that stage of the capitalist economy it was necessary to fabricate wants, otherwise you couldn't maintain the economy that would see great profit levels.[15] The gun propaganda was probably the beginning of it.

It continues to the Supreme Court's 2008 *Heller* decision.[16] What they call Second Amendment rights have just become holy writ. They're the most important rights that exist, our sacred rights to have guns, established by the Supreme Court, overturning a century of precedent.

Take a look at the Second Amendment. It says, "A well regulated Militia, being necessary to the security of a free State, the right of the people to keep and bear Arms, shall not be infringed." Up until 2008, that was interpreted pretty much the way it reads, that the point of having guns was to keep a militia. Justice Antonin Scalia, in his majority opinion in *Heller*, reversed that. He was a very good scholar. He's supposed to be an originalist and pay attention to the intentions of the Founders.

If you read the decision, it's interesting. There are all kinds of references to obscure seventeenth-century documents and so on. Strikingly, he never mentions once the reasons the Founders wanted the people to have guns, which are not obscure. One reason was that the British were coming. The British were the big enemy then. They were the most powerful state in the world. The United States barely had a standing army. If the British were going to come again, which in fact they did, you need militias to fight them off—so we have to have well-ordered militias.

The second reason is that the United States was a slave society. This was a period when slave rebellions were taking place all through the Caribbean. Slavery was growing massively after the American Revolution. At the time of the revolution, there were a couple hundred thousand slaves. By a couple decades later, it was maybe four million. So, there is a huge expansion of slavery, the most vicious system of slavery in history. There was deep concern. Black slaves often outnumbered whites. You had to have well-armed militias to keep them under control.

There was yet another reason. The United States is maybe one of the rare countries in history that has been at war virtually every year since its founding. You can hardly find a single year when the United States wasn't at war.

When you look back at the American Revolution, the textbook story focuses on "taxation without representation," which is not false but far from the whole story. Two major factors in the Revolution were that the British were imposing a restriction on expansion of settlement beyond the Appalachian Mountains into what was called "Indian country." The British were blocking that. The settlers wanted to expand to the west. Not just people who wanted land but also great land speculators, like George Washington, one of the leading ones, wanted to move into the western areas. "Western" meant right over the mountains. The British were blocking that. At the end of the war, the settlers could expand.

The other factor was slavery. In 1772, there was a very important and famous ruling by a leading British jurist, Lord Mansfield, that slavery is "so odious," his word, that it cannot be tolerated within Britain.[17] It could be tolerated in the colonies, like Jamaica, but not within Britain. The US colonies were essentially part of Britain. It was a slave society. They could see the handwriting on the wall. If the United States stays within the British system, it's going to be a real threat to slavery. That was ended by the Revolution.

So, that meant you needed guns to fend off the British; you needed them to control the slaves; you needed them to kill

Indians. If you're going to attack the Indian nations—they were nations, of course—you're going to attack the many nations to the west of the country, you're going to have to have guns and militias. Ultimately these were replaced later by a standing army.

But take a look at the reasons the Founders needed to have guns. Not a single˙one applies in the twenty-first century. This is completely missing not only from Scalia's decision but even from the legal debates over the Second Amendment.

There is a legal literature debating the *Heller* decision, but almost all of it is about the technical question of whether the Second Amendment is a militia right or an individual right. The wording of the amendment is a little bit ambiguous, so you can argue about it, but that's completely beside the point. The Second Amendment is totally irrelevant to the modern world. It has nothing to do with it, but it's holy writ.

So, you have this huge propaganda campaign. As a kid I was affected by it. Wyatt Earp, guns, kill Indians. Exciting! Everybody's been through it. It spread all over the world. The French love cowboy movies. This picture of the West is totally fabricated, but it was very successful in creating a gun culture. It's now become sanctified by the reactionary Supreme Court. So, yes, every body has to have guns.

People are terrified. The immigrants are coming across the border to kill us, so we'd better have a lot of assault rifles in the garage, just in case they're coming. The United States is a very frightened country.

I'd like you to talk about the First Amendment, press freedom, and journalism, a trade that has come under attack from the self-styled "extremely stable genius" in the White House as "the enemy of the people."[18]

The First Amendment is a major contribution of American democracy. The amendment actually doesn't guarantee the right of free speech. What it says is that the state cannot take preemptive action to prevent speech. It doesn't say it can't punish it. Nevertheless, the First Amendment was a step forward in the environment of the time that the United States in many ways did break through. With all of its flaws, the American Revolution was progressive in many respects by the standards of the time—even the phrase "We the people." Putting aside the flaws in implementation, the very idea was a breakthrough.

However, it wasn't really until the twentieth century that First Amendment issues really came on the agenda, at first with the dissenting opinions of Justices Oliver Wendell Holmes and Louis Brandeis in cases around the First World War and afterward. It's worth looking at how narrow these dissents were. The first major one, in *Schenck v. United States* in 1917, was a case of somebody who published a pamphlet describing the war as imperialist, arguing you don't have to serve in it. There was a dissenting opinion. However, the dissenter, Holmes, voted in favor of the punishment.

The right of free speech under the First Amendment was very narrow at first. In fact, the real steps toward establishing a strong protection of freedom of speech actually came in the 1960s. A major case was *New York Times [Company] v. Sullivan* in 1964. The State of Alabama had claimed what's called sovereign immunity, that you can't attack the state with words. That's a principle that holds in most countries—Britain, Canada, others. There was a civil rights movement ad that denounced the sheriff in Alabama for racist activities, and the state sued to block it. The ad was in the *Times*. That's why it's called *Times v. Sullivan*.

The case went to the Supreme Court. For the first time, basically, the court struck down the doctrine of sovereign immunity. It ruled that you can attack the state with words. Of course, it had been done before, but now it became legal.

There was a stronger decision a couple years later, *Brandenburg v. Ohio*, in 1969, in which the court ruled that speech should be free up to participation in an imminent criminal action. So, for example, if you and I go into a store with the intent to rob it, and you have a gun, and I say, "Shoot," that's not privileged. But that's basically the doctrine. That's a very strong protection of freedom of speech. There's nothing like it anywhere, as far as I know.

In practice, the United States doesn't have a stellar record but one of the better, maybe even the best record, in protection of freedom of speech and freedom of the press. That is indeed under attack when the president denounces the press as the "enemy of the people" and organizes a rabid support base to attack the press. That's a serious threat.

How do these protections apply to Julian Assange?

The real threat to Assange from the very beginning, the reason he took refuge in the Ecuadorian embassy in London, was the threat of extradition to the United States, now a reality.

He has already been charged with violations of the Espionage Act—so, theoretically, he can even be executed. Assange's crime has been to expose secret documents that are very embarrassing for state power. One of the main ones was the exposure of the video of pilots talking about how much fun they were having killing people.

In Baghdad.

Yes. But then there were a lot of others, some of them quite interesting. The press has reported them, of course. So, he's performing the journalistic responsibility of informing the public about information state power would rather keep secret.

It seems to be the essence of what a good journalist should be doing.

And what good journalists do. Like when Seymour Hersh exposed the story of the My Lai massacre and when Bob Woodward and Carl Bernstein exposed President Nixon's crimes. That was considered very praiseworthy. The *New York Times* published excerpts from the Pentagon Papers.

Assange is essentially doing something similar. You can question his judgment. Should he have done this at this time? Should he have done something else? There are lots of criticisms you can make. But the basic story is that WikiLeaks was publishing materials that state power wanted suppressed but that the public should know.

Talk about the present occupant of the White House. In some ways, his boorish and grotesque behavior is an easy target. People can feel very virtuous about denouncing Trump. But Public Citizen says we are witnessing a "slide toward authoritarianism" under Trump.[19] Are you concerned about that?

I'm less concerned than Public Citizen is. I think the system is resilient enough to withstand a figure who is defying subpoenas, defying congressional orders, and so on. I think Trump is in many ways underestimated. He's a highly skilled politician who is very successful in what he's doing.

Trump has two major constituencies. One is the actual, standard constituency of the Republican Party—both parties, but much more the Republicans—private wealth, corporate power. You've got to keep them satisfied. Then there is the voting base.

What's happened to the Republicans over the years is pretty interesting. Actually, during the neoliberal period, both parties have shifted to the right. By the 1970s, the Democrats had pretty much abandoned the working class. The last gesture of support for the working class was the Humphrey-Hawkins Act in 1978, a full employment bill that President Carter watered down so it didn't really mean anything. But since then, the Democrats have simply handed the working class over to their main class enemy, the Republicans.

The Democrats have become what used to be called moderate Republicans. The Republicans, meanwhile, have just gone off the edge. I think there is a lot of merit to the analysis of two scholars at the American Enterprise Institute, Thomas Mann and Norman Ornstein, who say the party has "become a radical insurgency."[20]

You see it almost daily. A couple days ago, Senator Mitch Mc-Connell said that if they have a chance to appoint someone else to the Supreme Court in an election year, they'll do it. When it was Obama, McConnell said, no, in an election year you can't do it.[21] They have simply abandoned any pretense of being a parliamentary party and upped it to the jugular. But meanwhile we're going to support private wealth, corporate power, with utter dedication.

You can't get votes that way, though. There are not enough people that are going to say, fine, let's do that.

What the Republicans have had to do since the 1970s is to try to cobble together a voting constituency on some grounds other than their actual policies. It's been very interesting to watch. It started with Nixon and his Southern strategy. The civil rights movement alienated southern racists. The Nixon team pretty openly said, we can pick up votes by being racist. They didn't use the word, but they were essentially catering to the racist elements of the South that are opposed to the civil rights movement.

It was then picked up by Paul Weyrich, one of the chief Republican strategists. He noticed in the mid-1970s that Republicans could get lots of votes if they pretended—stress *pretended*—to oppose abortion. The Republican Party had been almost completely pro-choice. Ronald Reagan, George Bush, Barry Goldwater, all of them, their position in the 1960s was basically that the state has nothing to say about abortion. It's a matter between a woman and her doctor. But Weyrich recognized that Republicans could get the votes of northern Catholics, workers, and evangelical Christians, who are a huge population in the United States, if they pretend to be antiabortion. Instantly they all became passionately opposed to abortion. That's now one of the leading planks of the Republican Party.

Guns is another central plank. We have to be pro-guns. We can pick up more voters this way. A good part of the population, especially the working class, has indeed suffered under the neoliberal programs instituted since the Reagan years. We can't tell people, look, we're screwing you, so we have to find some scape-goat who is responsible for your situation. In the case of Reagan, it was outright racist. The problem was Black welfare queens, the Black woman driving up in a limousine to the welfare office to steal your hard earned money. Now it's immigrants. The immigrants are coming to steal your jobs. Or China is going to take your job. It's kind of amazing to watch it work.

There's almost 100 percent agreement that China is taking our jobs. How is China taking our jobs? Does China have a gun to the heads of the CEOs of Apple and GM and Microsoft, demanding, "You've got to send jobs here"? It's corporate managers who are deciding to relocate operations to China. So, if you don't want jobs to go to China, you should be saying, "The corporate managers shouldn't have the right to make that decision." So, who should have the right? If you believe in democracy, the people who work in the enterprise. Where are we now? Back to the gentleman named Karl Marx in the mid-nineteenth century. We should have worker control of enterprises.

So, the logical argument about China stealing our jobs goes straight to workers' control of enterprises, the main theme of the US working class in the early Industrial Revolution. Somehow you don't read about that.

So, China is taking our jobs, immigrants are taking our jobs, welfare mothers are stealing from you, you have to have guns, you can't have abortions. They've had to cobble together a voting constituency including these sectors as well as the relatively affluent. Trump voters are mostly pretty affluent. They, of course, are going to vote Republican for their own reasons.

What's happened in the past roughly fifteen years, when you take a look at every Republican primary, when somebody came up from the popular base—people like Michele Bachmann, Rick Santorum, and others—they were so crazy that the Republican establishment wasn't able to tolerate them and was able to beat them down.

The difference in 2016 is they couldn't beat down Trump. He is a skillful politician who managed not only to win the nomination but to put the entire party in his pocket to a remarkable extent. Amazingly, he's been able to maintain the support of people that he is shafting at every turn with his pretense of being the guy who is standing up for you.

There was an interesting article a couple days ago in the *New York Times*, a long study of Midwest farmers. These are pretty affluent farmers, not poor farmers with a garden in their backyard. But they're suffering from the trade war. They're losing their market for soybeans. But they're still supporting Trump. And the reason is, we've got to stop the Chinese practices. It's unfair to us. And Trump says he supports us. In fact, the main person they quote in the article says he's going to vote for Trump because he said he "loves farmers."[22] So, a little sweet talk.

And also a little bit of cash doesn't hurt. So, there's now $16 billion sent to farmers in the Midwest to try to compensate for their trade losses. Where does that $16 billion come from? It comes from the trade war. Tariffs are simply a tax on consumers. That's what a tariff is. A tariff ends up with higher prices for consumers. And it's not small. The New York Federal Reserve Bank just estimated the annual tax bite as about $800 per family.[23] That's a big tax increase under Trump, which helps pay off his constituency.

It's a pretty nice scam, when you look at it, and they're carrying it off very effectively. He and Steve Bannon and the rest are pretending to be tribunes of the people, defending the American worker from all these attacks. By now there are a few Democrats who are starting to talk about this topic, but as a party the Democrats have pretty much abandoned the working class.

Many working people voted for Obama, believing his nice rhetoric about hope and change. But within about two years, that was shattered. By the 2010 midterm elections, it was gone. Working people are not going to vote for a guy who bails out the banks that cheated us and caused the crash, but doesn't notice the part of the congressional bailout legislation about helping the victims. Trump comes along and says, I'm your defender, I'm going to protect you from not only foreign enemies but also the people who are stealing your jobs. He's carrying it off. And the Democrats are helping him.

Take this laser-like focus on the Mueller report and Russiagate. It was obvious from the beginning that they were not going to find very much. They'll find that he's a crook—okay, we knew that already—but they're not going to find any real collusion with the Russians, and they didn't. They're not going to find any real significant Russian impact on the election. There couldn't be.

If you want to talk about interference with the election, campaign funding by the wealthy and the corporate sector utterly overwhelms the effect of any imaginable foreign interference. That's the real interference with elections. Whatever the Russians might have tried to do, it's a piece of straw in a haystack. And, of course, it's nothing compared with US interference with Russian elections, let alone in other countries, where we just overthrow the government. But the Democrats focused all their hopes on the idea that somehow Mueller is going to save us, and let's not look at Trump's policies.

The policies are murderous. Trump's climate policy may literally be a virtual death knell for the species. There's almost no talk about it. The Nuclear Posture Review, which escalates the threat of nuclear war significantly, that's not under discussion. Or the tax scam, which was just a gift to the rich and the corporations—a double gift. For one thing, it poured a lot of money into their pockets. Secondly, it created a huge deficit, which can be used as a justification for cutting social spending.

We can go on and on. None of this is being discussed. Let's talk about the fact that maybe somebody in the Trump campaign talked to a Russian oligarch who placed an ad somewhere. It's as if the Democrats are working for him, like paid agents of the Trump campaign.

Maureen Dowd, a columnist for the *New York Times*, writes, "My head hurts, puzzling over whether Trump is just a big blowhard who's flailing around, or a sinister genius laying traps to get himself impeached to animate the base ahead of the election."[24]

He's a narcissistic megalomaniac. That's pretty obvious. He understands nothing about the economy, he doesn't care about the world. But he is extremely skillful in carrying off the primary tasks that a narcissistic megalomaniac has to achieve. One is maintaining the support of wealth and corporate power, which he is doing. That's handed over to McConnell and the rest. They make sure that all works. And it's working brilliantly. Corporate profits are going through the roof. It's fantastic. Wages are pretty much stagnating. What more can we ask for? But the other thing is that he has to keep his voting base energized, and he's doing that very well.

Impeachment is another case. If the Democrats move to impeachment, I think they're going to shoot themselves in the foot. You can see exactly what's going to happen. Suppose the House impeaches Trump. It goes to the Senate. The Senate is in Trump's pocket. They'll exonerate him. Then what happens? Trump starts making speeches about how "I'm exonerated. The Deep State and the treacherous Democrats are trying to destroy the guy who is standing up for you against your enemies." Just like what happened with the Mueller report. They were just walking into a trap.

If you want to be concerned, you want to overturn Trump on the basis of his actual crimes, the thing to look at is not Congress but the New York State Attorney General's office, which is carrying out, apparently, careful investigations of Trump's fraudulent dealings over decades, which I'm sure are going to pile up crime after crime, maybe enough to send him to prison after he's out of office.

But the fraud with his hotels and so on, that's very minor as compared with the fact that he's escalating the race to disaster. This is the most important decision in human history. We've got a couple of years to try to deal somehow with an environmental crisis. It can be controlled. It's not easy, but it can be done. If you waste a couple of years by trying to escalate the crisis, you might just push us over the edge.

I don't know if you've looked at this, one of the most amazing documents in human history, that came out of the Trump administration, from a part of the bureaucracy, naturally. It was a five-hundred-page environmental assessment study by the Transportation Department, the point of which was to argue that we should not impose new emissions controls on cars and trucks.[25] And they had a very sound argument. The argument is, look, we're going off the cliff anyway, and car emissions don't make that much of a difference. So, who cares? Their estimate was that by the end of this century, global temperatures will have risen 4 degrees centigrade. That's way beyond what the scientific consensus says will make life virtually unlivable. So, what they're saying is, we're finished, it's all done anyhow, by the end of the century everything will be destroyed. So why stop driving? Can you think of anything like this in human history, ever?

Of course, they're assuming that everyone is as criminally insane as we are—and that nobody is going to do anything about it.

All of this passes without anybody paying attention. Let's worry about whether Russia had some minor influence on the election.

Could you talk about the young people in Congress like Alexandria Ocasio-Cortez, Ilhan Omar, Rashida Tlaib, Ayanna Pressley, and others, and teen activist students like Greta Thunberg of Sweden, Haven Coleman of Denver, Colorado, and the young people involved in Extinction Rebellion and the Sunrise Movement?

That's very exciting. That's really the hope for the future. These are very impressive people. Extinction Rebellion are great people. The

Sunrise Movement, which is, after all, a small group of young people, succeeded partly just through their activism, like sitting in in congressional offices, with support from especially Ocasio-Cortez, who is doing a wonderful job.

They managed to put the Green New Deal on the agenda. Now, of course, it's immediately been denounced as crazy, but it's a great achievement. There has to be some kind of Green New Deal if we're going to survive. And they managed to move it from obscurity to the legislative agenda, along with Ed Markey, the senator from Massachusetts. That's a real achievement.

There are very solid, substantive proposals as to how you could implement these plans. One of the most detailed and persuasive I know of is by Robert Pollin, an economist at UMass Amherst.[26] It can be done. These groups have broken through the silence and apathy on it. That's a remarkable achievement.

In fact, it's the hope for survival of any kind of civilized life. This is not a small thing. The human species is facing questions that have never arisen before. Is organized human life going to survive in any recognizable form? We're approaching the level of global warming of roughly 125,000 years ago, when sea levels were about twenty to twenty-five feet higher than they are now. You don't have to have much of an imagination to know what that means.

Well, shall we race toward our destruction the way the Trump administration and the Republican Party want us to do? Or shall we do something about it, the way the Sunrise Movement, Extinction Rebellion, and Ocasio-Cortez want to do? That's the decision.

THREATS TO PEACE AND THE PLANET

Pima Community College, Tucson, Arizona   November 4, 2019

Good evening, Tucson. It's wonderful to see you all here. It's an honor to be here and to be with someone I have been working closely with for many years, and who is actually responsible for my radio program, *Alternative Radio*. Because when I first became familiar with his work, I was really surprised that Chomsky was rarely heard on community radio stations and public radio stations across the country, so I wanted to rectify that. That was the beginning of *Alternative Radio*. We have more than two hundred and fifty recordings of Noam in our vast audio archive—lectures and interviews and debates.

So, Noam, you have a lot to answer for in terms of your supporting independent community radio. And thank you for that.

My greatest achievement [*laughs*].

Let's start with the *Economist*, not necessarily a radical journal. In its current issue, the *Economist* observes, there's "something in the air" and asks, "Why are so many countries witnessing mass protests?"[1] Then it goes on to write about the many countries where people are demonstrating in great numbers, from Santiago, Chile, to Beirut, Lebanon, to Sudan, to Hong Kong, Haiti, and Iraq. What is prompting this massive upsurge in popular activism?

Well, of course, each country you look at has its own particular-
ities and special reasons, but there are some common features,
which were actually captured pretty well by a young demon-
strator in Chile whose comment became a slogan for the huge
demonstrations: "It's not about 30 pesos, it's about 30 years."[2]
That's roughly the period of the neoliberal programs that took
over much of the world, the United States and other countries.
They've had pretty deleterious effects for the general population.
It's different in different countries, and there are other factors,
but this is common.

We can see very well what this has led to in the United States.
The United States has one of the more vibrant economies in the
modern world. Nevertheless, most of the population says they
don't have good jobs and they live very precarious lives.

If you look at the statistics behind this, more than half the
population has negative net worth, meaning debts exceeding assets, with very little to carry them over if any unexpected development happens, an accident or anything else. Meanwhile 0.1
percent of the population—not 1 percent; 0.1 percent—have more
than 20 percent of the country's wealth, and that's accelerating.
The tendency has increased since the Great Recession. Benefits
have declined.

The United States is pretty extreme in this respect among
all the Organisation for Economic Co-operation and Development (OECD) countries, the rich countries. It's the only one that
doesn't have some form of national health care. The result is that
health care costs about twice as high as the average and has out-
comes that are relatively poor.

For the first time in more than a century, mortality is increasing.[3] Mortality is increasing particularly among the basically
working-age sector of the white population, roughly people who
are twenty-five to fifty years old. That hasn't happened anywhere
in a developed society since the huge flu epidemic a century ago.

There is concentration of wealth at the top while there is essentially stagnation for the majority of the population. So, the purchasing power of real wages today is about what it was in the 1970s, before this assault took place. One of the consequences of concentration of wealth is almost the increased power of extreme wealth and the corporate sector over the political system. That happens almost automatically.

So, there has been a decline in functioning democracy. People feel that the government is not responsive to them. They're correct. They don't have to read political science journals to discover that about 70 percent of the population is essentially disenfranchised. That is, if you're in the lower 70 percent in the wealth scale, if you compare opinions and attitudes, which we know a lot about from polls, with the voting records of their representatives, there's essentially no correlation. The representatives are listening to other voices. The other voices are the donor class for the next election. When somebody is elected to Congress, the first thing that he or she has to do is start working on getting funding for the next round. Representatives may spend five or six hours a day just talking to donors.

Meanwhile, something is happening in their offices. There's been a huge explosion of lobbyists during this neoliberal period. They go to congressional offices and sit with the staff. The staff are nice people, but they're overwhelmed by the information, true or false, the expertise, legal backgrounds of this mass of lobbyists, who pretty much write the legislation, which the representatives then sign. It's naturally going to have little relation to the people who voted the representatives into office.

This is felt by people. They know the government doesn't represent them.

It's in many ways even worse in Europe. In Europe, where you have the same economic issues, expanded by the austerity programs, even worse than here, the structure of the European Union transfers essential decision-making away from people and national governments, where they have some influence, to an unelected bureaucracy in Brussels—the European Commission, unelected, the International Monetary Fund, the European Central Bank, with the German banks looking over their shoulders. People feel, rightly, that they have no role in the political system. And while they're suffering from the economic policies, great wealth is rapidly accumulating.

One or another variant of this is happening over much of the world. It has obvious consequences. People get angry and dissatisfied, resentful. They begin to despise the more or less centrist institutions that have been running the world during most of their lives. In Europe, the centrist parties, the center-left, center-right parties, are basically collapsing. The Social Democratic Party in Germany, which goes back to about the mid-nineteenth century, has virtually disappeared, and the Christian Democrats are sharply declining. You're seeing a rise in fringe parties.

Pretty much the same is happening here. Because of our political system, the parties keep their names, but they're changing their character in the same way. In fact, there are some recent studies of the political parties in the Western world, looking at their political programs and ranking them on a spectrum from what's called left to right. The Democratic Party here is sort of right in the center. It's with the centrist parties of other countries. The Republican Party is just off the spectrum. They're ranked alongside fringe parties in Europe, the parties that have sort of neofascist roots.

The most striking feature of the 2016 election was that the center collapsed. If you look at the Republican primaries for the last roughly fifteen to twenty years, every time a candidate emerged from the base, they were so intolerable to the establishment that they were just crushed by the concentrated power and force of the Republican establishment: Michele Bachmann, Herman Cain, Rick Santorum. The big difference was they couldn't do it in 2016. They got somebody who did arise from the base, and they couldn't destroy him.

In the Democratic Party primaries, something similar occurred. Bernie Sanders broke with over a century of US political history by rising up to the point of nomination without any support from the standard array of funders, those who buy the elections—the corporate sector and extreme wealth—with no media - support. He might very well have been nominated if it hadn't been for the machinations of party managers. That's unheard of in US political history. But it's essentially the same phenomenon, coming from the population. Trump came from another part of the population.

When you look around the world, you find one or another variant of this. There are special issues. So, in Brazil, which is quite a striking phenomenon, the leading political figure, Inácio Lula da Silva, was about to win the election a year ago. There is a kind of an elite soft coup that's been going on for several years, and they handled this by simply putting him in jail on very dubious charges. Furthermore, not only putting him in jail but barring him from making any public statement, unlike mass murderers, for example. So, he was silenced, put in jail.

A huge social media campaign began. We're going to see more of this in the next year. It had Steve Bannon's fingerprints all over it. Most Brazilians get their information, as it's called, from social media. It was swamped with the most incredible campaign of lies, vilification, and defamation and accusations of a most incredible sort. It frightened people about the opposition, and it scared them into electing a real monstrous figure, Jair Bolsonaro.

Take a look at Lebanon. The corruption of the elites is indescribable. One of the main charges against the prime minister is that he gave $16 million to some South African model he was having an affair with. Meanwhile, the trash isn't being picked up. On top of this, there is a confessional system that was imposed by France when they were the colonial power. When they left in the

1940s, they made a deal among the Christian, Sunni, and Shi'a populations about how they apportioned governance. There hasn't been any census since then, and the Shi'a are very much underrepresented. This system is formally a democracy, but it prevents serious democratic functioning. So that's a major issue.

But in this atmosphere of anger and resentment, frustration, contempt for institutions, it's very fertile territory for demagogues to come along and to say, Your problem is not the corporate sectors or the wealthy or the people who are making the policies. It's somebody who is even more vulnerable than you—immigrants, Muslims, African Americans, Ronald Reagan's welfare queens. Just look around and find somebody to blame.

There's pretty good evidence by now, a lot of studies, that the xenophobia and the fury against immigrants and so on tends to follow economic policies that are cutting back benefits, making wages stagnate, and so on. This is true even in countries like Sweden. You see a rise in xenophobia, anger, pathological symptoms of various kinds. Almost always it follows after the economic policies that are associated with the whole neoliberal system. That's kind of the underlying background for what's happening.

What's happening in the Amazon in terms of fires and environmental destruction?

Bolsonaro, the president who was just elected, has basically given carte blanche to agribusiness, logging, and mineral industries, his constituency, telling them, just burn it up and use it for grazing, mineral extraction, anything you want.

There is a certain problem about that. The Amazon is very fragile. These are short-term gains, and the forest isn't coming back. Meanwhile, it has regional and, in fact, global effects. I'm sure you've often heard the Amazon described as the lungs of the Earth. It is responsible for an enormous amount of carbon removal from the atmosphere. It's the basis for the ecology of the South American region. It's the place where water condenses and leads to the heavy rains that permit agricultural development. And then, of course, for the whole world that means a blow against the very perilous efforts to try to do something about the ecological catastrophe that's looming.

My wife, Valéria, happens to be Brazilian. The two of us were visiting Brazil a couple of months ago. In São Paulo, at three in the afternoon on a nice sunny day, all of a sudden it became pitch black, literally like midnight. Nobody knew what was happening. Well, it turned out that the fires in the Amazon, far away, were creating so much smoke that they darkened the skies and turned bright mid-afternoon into midnight. That's a vivid indication of the kinds of things that are happening, but it's happening mostly out of sight.

Associated with this is essentially extermination of the indigenous populations that live in those areas. As the loggers and miners move into the areas, they want to get rid of the people. We're kind of familiar with that in our own history. The indigenous people who have been the kind of caretakers of the forests and live in close interaction with them are being decimated and threatened with destruction.

Among his outlandish pronouncements, Bolsonaro has said that the indigenous population should be eliminated.[4] He said that what they really want is iPhones and to be begging and to be homeless in the cities, not to live in their own areas that are designated for them. So, let's just get rid of them. Bolsonaro is very supportive of the military. In fact, he claims that the military dictatorship didn't even take place; it was just saving the country from a communist takeover.[5] Totally fanciful. The dictatorship was harsh and brutal.

But he has criticized the military. He's criticized them on two grounds. One, he said they're too soft. They should have done what the Argentine military did at roughly the same time—killed thirty thousand people. But the Brazilian military didn't do that, and now we have this problem of these people around who should have been murdered. He also criticized the nineteenth-century

Brazilian military because they didn't behave like the cavalry in the United States and exterminate the native population. If they had done that, Brazil wouldn't have this problem of indigenous people.[6]

So, the Amazon is under very severe threat. Actually, my wife is trying to compensate for it by recreating a small model of the Amazon by planting Brazilian trees in our yard in Tucson.

That military dictatorship lasted from 1964 to 1985.

That dictatorship is worth knowing about. There was a kind of plague of repression that spread over the whole continent, beginning in the early 1960s. The Brazilian dictatorship was the first. It was lauded by the United States. Ambassador Lincoln Gordon hailed the overthrow of the government and the establishment of the dictatorship as one of the greatest moments of "freedom" in the "mid-twentieth century."[7] Investors poured in. Capital poured in. It was considered a wonderful event—a brutal, vicious, neo-Nazi-style dictatorship. Then others spread around the continent. Our own role in that is not very pretty, if you look at it. It's worth looking at carefully.

My parents were immigrants. Your father was an immigrant. Your mother came here at a very young age. Was she born in the United States?

She was one year old when she came.

We're sitting here in Tucson, sixty miles from the Mexican border. Things are going on there that can scarcely be believed—not just there but all across the country—with the setting up of detention camps and the separation of children from parents. How is the administration in Washington getting away with this? Where is the indignation and anger?

Actually, here in Tucson, there is a reaction, a courageous reaction. People like the No More Deaths group, for example, and others are reacting properly. And they do have a fair amount of popular support here. But it's true that it's not happening around the country. We can find out why easily.

I don't know how many of you read the online *Tucson Sentinel*, a pretty good newspaper, actually. They had a very interesting report probably one or two months ago.[8] Steve Bannon was visiting the area. He was going to a luxurious gated community south of Tucson. The goal was to raise money to privately build a wall because the government isn't doing it. A reporter got into the meeting somehow and gave a careful description of people's reactions, which were pretty interesting. People in this rich, gated community, which is probably the most secure place in the entire world, are terrified. They're afraid that an invasion is coming of rapists, murderers, Islamic terrorists who are going to carry out genocide against the white race, and they've got to do something about it.

One of the people there, a former representative from Colorado, actually, suggested that Arizona not only build a wall at the border but also at the California border, because we don't want those people coming here. [*Audience laughter*] We can laugh at this, but this is real. People are really frightened and terrified.

This is an old story in the United States. It's been the most secure country in the world since the War of 1812, but it's probably one of the most frightened countries in the world. It's very easy to arouse the population to extreme fear. That's happened over and over.

In recent years, you will recall the propaganda to build up support for the invasion of Iraq was effective. People were afraid. We've got to stop Saddam before he kills us. If you take a look at international polls, there was almost no support for the invasion, practically nothing. It barely reached 10 percent anywhere. In the United States, though, the fear was real. When Condoleezza Rice said, "We don't want the smoking gun to be a mushroom cloud," people didn't laugh.[9]

You see the propaganda every day that Iran is the greatest threat to world peace. They're going to attack us. We've got to prevent them from doing this. People don't collapse in laughter.

They take it seriously. If you take a look at the facts, it's beyond ridicule. But it goes on because people are afraid.

When we last talked, you said that if the Democrats move to impeachment, "they're going to shoot themselves in the foot." You called impeachment "a trap." The Democrats have formally moved on impeachment. Have your views changed?

Well, we don't know for certain. Your guess is as good as mine. But my expectation is that the House will impeach, the Senate will reject it. I doubt very much that you can find enough Republican senators with a bit of principle. They all know that Trump is impeachable one hundred times over. But do they want to face Trump's adoring, militant base? Not many will.

If you think about election interference, it's pretty hard to take seriously. Suppose there were some Russian interference. It would be almost invisible in comparison to the huge interference of simply buying elections. There's very extensive and very convincing work showing that electability to the presidency or Congress is very highly predictable from the single variable of campaign spending. Thomas Ferguson, a great political scientist, has been publishing on this for years. He just came out a couple of days ago with a new paper, which is a very careful analysis of congressional elections over about, I think, forty years.[10] The predictability is just incredible. That's massive interference with elections. It's gotten much worse in recent years because of the decisions of the reactionary Supreme Court, but it goes way back.

That's why the Sanders achievement was so spectacular. It broke with this, but in the face of that kind of interference with elections, which is just the beginning, I should say.

There is an insidious organization, American Legislative Exchange Council (ALEC), which kind of operates quietly but has the support of a wide range of the corporate system, really across the board. What they're doing is quite clever. They're trying to impose legislation at the state level, and succeeding.

What happens at the state level is very important for people's lives, but people don't know much about it. Most people can't name their state representative. It's not reported, you don't pay any attention to it. It's just something that happens out there. And state legislators are much easier to buy than congressional representatives. It doesn't take much money to win a state election. So, ALEC is imposing identical legislative programs in states throughout the country to turn the country into an ultra-reactionary society at the state level.

Incidentally, Arizona was singled out in one of their campaigns to try to destroy the public education system. They want to do that everywhere. The public education system is just too democratic. And there are many ways to undermine it, like defunding and so on. But they're trying to literally privatize it. They thought that Arizona would be kind of a soft spot—maybe they could ram it through here.

Other things they're doing are almost unimaginable. For example, there are billions of dollars every year of stolen wages. It's called wage theft. Employers simply don't pay their workers, or if they work overtime, they don't give them what they're due. One of ALEC's main programs is to try to prevent even investigation of this, let alone punishment for it. And they do it at the state level, one after another.

One of their most insidious programs is to try to get states to vote for a constitutional amendment for a balanced budget. You know what that means. A balanced budget at the federal level means you pour money into the Pentagon, pour money into subsidies for the energy corporations, and cut everything else. That's what's called a balanced budget. If that becomes a constitutional amendment, the effects are horrifying. And they're getting pretty close to the number of states to do it. All under the radar—not many people know about it.

And we talk about a tiny possible Russian influence somewhere. It's a joke.

Quite apart from the fact that the United States intervenes massively in elections all over the world perfectly openly, even overthrowing governments. Also in Russia. In 1996, the Clinton administration very much wanted Boris Yeltsin, their man, to be elected president of Russia. He was running badly in the polls, but they poured expertise and money into it and managed to win the election for him. It wasn't secret. They were proud of it.

In the face of all of this, for us to be talking about the Russian or Chinese or Cuban or whatever influence in US elections is another sign of this same kind of paranoia that shows up in the gated community when they think they have to be protected from an invasion from across the border.

We're not the only country in history where the population has been deluded by massive propaganda. Just think about Germany. It's very striking. In the 1920s, Germany was the absolute peak of Western civilization. In the sciences, in the arts, it was considered the leading political democracy in the world, had a very rich tradition. Ten years later, it was the absolute depths of human history. Ten years after that, it's becoming a significant civilized cultural center again.

Joseph Goebbels, who was Hitler's propaganda minister and regarded as a kind of brilliant strategist, said, even though negative things were being said about Hitler and the Nazis, "the main thing is, they're talking about us."[11]

You've described the present occupant of the Oval Office as a "narcissistic megalomaniac," which is rather unusual for you.[12] You usually don't label politicians so baldly as that. But all the attention that's being focused on him seems to energize him even more.

It's by now pretty well recognized that the major television networks gave him a tremendous gift in the 2016 election campaign. And they, as you recall, bragged about it.

Leslie Moonves, the head of CBS.

He's the greatest thing that ever happened to our ratings, he said.

He said, the Trump campaign "may not be good for America, but it's damn good for CBS . . . . The money's rolling in."[13]

They were giving Trump huge propaganda. Of course, he relishes that. The Trump administration is often described as a kind of fascism, which is a little bit glib. It doesn't rise to the level of fascism. Fascism, remember, had an ideology, the ideology of a powerful state under the control of a single party that controls the whole society. It controls not only labor but business and everything else. We are very far from that. We don't have that ideology. Also, fascism uses force and violence to impose its will.

But some of the kind of appurtenances of fascism do appear here. One of them is the destruction of the information system. And this is not done just by propaganda. It's done, whether consciously or not, in a very effective way by just eliminating the notion of truth. Just flood the information system with massive lies and deceit, anything that comes to mind when you're, in Trump's case, watching Fox News in the morning and tweeting it out. It doesn't matter what it is. Say anything. Then the fact checkers in the *Washington Post* will write an article saying Trump told eighty-three lies this morning—but it doesn't make any difference, because it's cheapening the concept of truth and fact so that people have no idea what to believe. Fact and truth don't exist. It's a technique of propaganda that's extremely effective. It's working, and the effects are lethal.

I don't have to tell you that you we're facing a major crisis of an environmental catastrophe, and a large part of the population here simply refuses to believe it. After all, their leader tells them every day it's not happening, and they adore their leader, the man who stands up for them, so he claims, while shafting most of them at every turn. But he's the leader. We have to follow him. If he says it's not happening, it's not happening.

The last figures I saw, I think about a quarter of Republicans regarded global warming as a serious issue. Many don't even believe it's happening. The consequences of that are beyond words. Unless this changes, and changes very soon, we don't have to bother talking about anything else, because organized human society will disappear within a short period of time. That's what we're facing.

I should say that there is another existential threat, which we all know about in the back of our minds, but, again, almost no attention is being paid to it. We now have seventy-five years of living under the threat of nuclear catastrophe. It's almost a miracle that we've survived, just looking at the record. Now the threat is escalating. The United States is dismantling all of its arms control treaties. The second Bush administration got rid of one of them, the Anti-Ballistic Missile Treaty, which is quite important. An antiballistic missile sounds defensive, but it's well understood that it's basically a first-strike weapon. It's not going to deter a first-strike attack. It could conceivably deter a limited or retaliatory strike. So, that's gone.

Trump just pulled out of the Intermediate-Range Nuclear Forces Treaty, the Reagan-Mikhail Gorbachev treaty that greatly improved the security situation in Europe and the world by banning short-range missiles. The Trump administration was planning for this. Immediately after pulling out of the treaty in early August, they carried out a test of a missile, which violates the treaty, meaning it was already in development and being planned. It apparently happens to use pretty much the same technology that the Russians have been complaining about in the intercontinental ballistic missile installations on their borders. This just was saying to Vladimir Putin, please develop weapons that can destroy us.

And the military industry is just celebrating. They're euphoric, getting all kinds of fat contracts to develop hypersonic missiles, all sorts of unimaginable lethal weapons against which there is no defense. They're also looking forward, if you read their propaganda handouts, to the contracts to develop defenses against the weapons they are creating today, which, of course, others will carry out and develop, too.

The Trump administration has indicated that it doesn't plan to sign the New START Treaty if it's reelected. That comes up shortly after the election. The New START Treaty had been very effective. It's sharply reduced the number of missiles and warheads that the United States and Russia have, which doesn't end the problem but reduces it. They want to get rid of that and open the door to just massive overproduction of missiles and warheads, which threatens our survival, of course.

Right now, it looks as if John Bolton's last shot before he was kicked out of the administration was to initiate a breaking of the Open Skies Treaty. That was initiated by Eisenhower, who recognized that if Russia and the United States have ways of carrying out surveillance over the other's territory with joint participation, each will be safer, because they will know if the other is planning some aggressive act. That's been extremely effective. It looks like the Trump administration is going to throw it out, which again raises the threat enormously.

A little while ago, William Perry, a former defense secretary, who has spent his whole life on nuclear issues—a very serious, sober guy, not given to exaggeration—said that he was terrified at the rising threat of nuclear war and that he was doubly terrified because nobody was paying attention to it aside from the arms control community.[14] Actually, we can add something to that. We should be triply terrified by the rising threat, by the lack of attention—there's barely a word anywhere—and by the fact that it's being conducted by people who know exactly what they're doing: they understand perfectly well that they're sharply increasing the risk of destruction. That's an amazing phenomenon.

It's also true of the environmental catastrophe. The people who are exacerbating it understand perfectly well what they're doing. Exxon Mobil is the most famous case. The Exxon Mobil scientists in the 1960s and 1970s were in the lead in determining the nature of the threat and its seriousness, informing management of this terrible crisis that's coming from the use of oil. In 1988, James Hansen, a prominent geophysicist, gave a famous speech in which he warned the public about this danger.[15] Exxon Mobil management reacted to that by starting to fund denialism—not outright denialism because they don't want to just refute it, but sowing doubt, saying, "We don't really know." We shouldn't act too precipitously. Maybe there's something about clouds that we haven't understood. That's pretty effective, because it's pretty hard to counter. They knew exactly what they were doing.

Rex Tillerson, for example, who was CEO of Exxon Mobil at the time; the head of the big banks; JPMorgan Chase CEO Jamie Dimon, who knows as much as any of us do about the extremely grave threat of global warming—how are they reacting? Pouring funds into fossil fuel extraction.

Our leaders in the economic, political domain understand exactly what they're doing and race forward to do it in an even more extreme way.

Let me ask you about tactics. Let's say I totally agree with you on the impending environmental catastrophe and how that is being generated by predatory corporate capitalism. But then you find out that I'm against gay marriage, I'm against reproductive rights, I'm a misogynist, I'm a racist. Are you going to work with me toward a goal? How do you negotiate that?

There is just no choice. This matter is so urgent, as is nuclear war, that you have to make whatever alliances you can.

Actually, there was an interesting op-ed article in the *New York Times* a couple days ago by an evangelical Christian who was describing the kinds of tactics she thinks ought to be used to help the evangelical community recognize the importance of doing something urgent about global warming.[16] As you may know, about 80 percent of them support Trump. Her proposal was perfectly reasonable. She said, "By beginning with what we share and then connecting the dots between that value and a changing climate, it becomes clear how caring about this planet and every living thing on it is not somehow antithetical to who we are as Christians, but rather central to it. Being concerned about climate change is a genuine expression of our faith, bringing our attitudes and actions more closely into line with who we already are and what we most want to be."

Let's approach evangelical Christians that way. Is that wrong? I think that's quite right.

It's true that environmental destruction is simply inherent in the capitalist system of maximizing growth and profit, ignoring externalities. But it doesn't help. Maybe we should work to eliminate the system, but you look at the time scale of making radical social changes in institutions and doing something about the urgent environmental crisis, and the two just don't match. Responding to urgent environmental crisis has to dominate. Overcoming the crisis is going to have to be done within some form of existing institutions. It doesn't mean that you shouldn't be trying to change them, just as you should be dealing with misogyny. But this, along with nuclear war, overwhelms everything.

There are plenty of other problems, I should say. The problem of resistance to microbes—that could be a lethal problem in the not too distant future.

Because of global warming.

Partly that, but also because of their mutations. Say, industrial meat production, that uses maybe half the antibiotics in the country. That leads to very rapid evolution of microbes that are resistant to any form of microbial control we have. It's happening in hospitals. This is leading to development of possible plagues that we'll have no way of dealing with.

There may be things coming from global warming, too. So, one of the things that nobody knows anything about—but there are fears of—is that, as the permafrost melts in the Arctic's vast northern regions, it releases a huge amount of carbon, far beyond what's been released so far.[17]

Methane.

Methane, but also just plain carbon. The amount of carbon stored there is fantastic. But also, nobody knows what's down there. There may be bacteria that have been preserved for eons to which there is no resistance. It could happen.

Some were startled by your advocating for a small US troop presence in northern Syria along the Turkish border in the so-called Rojava area, the autonomous Kurdish state that had been established in that area. What was your thinking behind that?

You have to understand that human life isn't an axiom system. We don't have absolute principles that apply in every situation. Human life is much more complicated than that. There are conflicting values, and you have to consider the human consequences of the choices you're making in particular situations.

So, let's take this one. There was a small US contingent, a couple hundred soldiers, in the Kurdish areas, which was a deterrent against a Turkish invasion. If you look at the background, the Turkish government is carrying out extremely harsh repression and massacres of its Kurdish population inside Turkey. This goes way back, incidentally. Turkey invaded Syria already, took over part of Syria, extended the repression there—ethnic cleansing, massacres, and so on. Turkey wants to move on to other Kurdish-dominated areas.

What's going to happen if they do? Well, we could speculate before. Now we can see it. Exactly what was predicted. Further ethnic cleansing, further massacres. That was being deterred by a small US contingent that basically had no other function except backing up the Kurdish war against ISIS.

Trump likes to say that he defeated ISIS. Actually, it's the Kurds who defeated ISIS, with some US support in the back.

There were eleven thousand Kurds, men and women, killed in the fight, six Americans.[18] The US Special Forces were backing up the fight and US airpower was, of course, used, but the fighting on the ground was done by the Kurds. They're the ones who, with a Tweet in the morning, Trump decided to just hand over to their bitter enemies, to Turkey and to the Assad government.

Fortunately for them, Russia moved in. You're not supposed to say anything nice about Russia here, but in that region they happen to be the moderating force that's leading to some kind of diplomatic settlement. Maybe we don't like it, but it's a lot better than continuing this horrendous war, which is destroying Syria. And the Russians apparently have moved in to restrict the Turkish invasion. So maybe it won't be as bad as could have been forecast, but it's already pretty bad.

I don't see any problem with having had a deterrent US force there at the time. I think we should be careful not to turn our principles into a catechism that applies no matter what the circumstances. Life just doesn't allow that.

And this isn't the first time the United States has betrayed the Kurds.

Oh, God, no. It's practically a qualification for a president, literally. It's hard to find one. Back to Gerald Ford, in fact. Every single president, often in awful ways.

Like Reagan, for example. When Saddam Hussein, whom the United States was supporting at the time, carried out major massacres of Kurds in northern Iraq, chemical warfare attacks killing hundreds, thousands of people, Reagan tried to deflect the blame to Iran. When Congress was trying to respond in some way, Reagan actually vetoed their effort. Then later, when the United States decided to invade Iraq, they used this massacre of the Kurds as part of the basis for the invasion. How can we let somebody like that survive, who has carried out the Halabja massacre with chemical weapons? The cynicism is unbelievable.

Take Clinton. The Turkish repression of the Kurds inside Turkey has a very ugly history. The peak of the repression was in the 1990s. How did the Clinton administration react? By sharply increasing the flow of military aid to the Turkish government that was carrying out the atrocities. As the atrocities rose, military aid rose. In 1997, another peak of atrocities, Clinton sent more aid in that one year than all of US military aid to Turkey from the beginning of the Cold War up to the onset of the counterinsurgency. Almost nobody knew about it here. There was very little reporting. The news bureaus had, of course, offices in Ankara, staffed by good journalists. They weren't reporting it.

The population here in the United States, we're told repeatedly, is polarized. What do you think about someone who has a media diet not of *The Progressive* magazine or listening to *Alternative Radio* or watching *Democracy Now!* but Fox, Breitbart News, Infowars, *RedState*, Newsmax, and all those other very narrow points of view? How do you reach those people?

First of all, when people talk about the country being polarized or the political system being polarized, it's a little misleading. The Democrats, the roughly liberal population, are pretty much centrist. The political party of the Democrats is not very different from what moderate Republicans used to be. If you read the *New York Times*, you get a fair range of opinion, from moderate center-left over to far right. It's all there. But when you turn to Fox News or Breitbart or something, that's different. Then you're in an invented world way off to the right. So, the polarization is not mutual—it's unidirectional. But it does lead to a sharply divided population.

How do you reach the people? The way this evangelical professor described it. You don't reach them by ridicule, hatred, or anger, but by recognizing that, somewhere down there, we have a common humanity—and you've got to find that and work from there.

I was in Kansas City recently, and learned more about *Appeal to Reason*. This was a weekly socialist newspaper that, astonishingly, had a subscription base of 450,000 in 1910. I wish *The Progressive* magazine had that many subscribers today. Its writers included Upton Sinclair, Jack London, Mother Jones, Eugene Debs, and Helen Keller. That's just one example of a past that is largely hidden from view.

We have other examples. Kansas and Oklahoma are states that you would think are on the extreme right, and always have been historically. But that's not the case at all. In 1914, Oklahoma had 175 elected socialist officials in the state.

When Eugene Victor Debs first ran for president in 1900 as the Socialist Party candidate, he received fewer than ninety thousand votes. In 1920, while he was imprisoned in Atlanta, he received almost a million votes.

Today, socialism is being denounced by the occupant in the Oval Office—"It's never going to happen in the United States"—but because of Alexandria Ocasio-Cortez and Bernie Sanders, the word has been injected into the political discourse again. What do you think about the possibilities of a socialist outcome?

What you say is quite correct. In fact, the most radical democratic movement in US history was the populist movement. I have to say, I shudder when I hear the word *populism* being used today. It has nothing to do with traditional populism. The populist movement was a movement that started with farmers in Texas and moved through the Midwest—Kansas, Oklahoma, Wisconsin—up to the north. A major movement with very radical policies.

The populists wanted to get rid of the northern bankers who were demanding usurious payments. They wanted cooperatively owned banks, cooperative organization of the market. Basically, developing a socialist society at the base. A huge movement. They were just beginning to link up with the Knights of Labor, the first major labor movement. Again, a very huge, mostly urban-based movement, which had radical political goals. One of their slogans was that "those who work in the mills should own them."

It's hard to remember, maybe, but a slogan of the Republican Party back in the mid-nineteenth century, Lincoln's Republican Party, was that there is no difference between wage labor and slavery, except that wage labor is temporary. But no one should be at the command of a master. That's intolerable. That was the view of working people, in their press and so on.

There is a very rich radical background in the country, far beyond what Bernie Sanders and Elizabeth Warren or anybody is talking about. In fact, what's called socialism today is sort of New Deal liberalism, maybe extended. The programs and policies that Sanders is advocating wouldn't really have surprised President Eisenhower very much. When you read Eisenhower's statements about labor rights or the New Deal, he said that any political figure who doesn't accept the New Deal and support the right of workers to unionize doesn't belong in our political system. That's not Sanders, that's Eisenhower. The country has shifted so far to the right that what looks like a radical, revolutionary position used to be the norm.

As you mentioned, among the many forms of US exceptionalism, so-called, is that the word *socialism*, which usually means moderate social democracy, has become a curse word. That's not true anywhere else. If somebody somewhere else says, "He's a socialist"—or, for that matter, "a communist"—it just means you're kind of on the critical edge of the political system. Here it's been turned into a four-letter word. You can't utter it. So, Sanders seems to be breaking all kinds of rules when he uses a word that is standard everywhere else.

Gabriel Kolko, a great historian who died a couple years ago, has a very interesting book called *Main Currents in Modern American History*.[19] It's very much worth reading. One of the things Kolko argues is that, after the populist movement in the United States was pretty much crushed by force, many of the radical farmers just left for Canada and formed the basis of the Canadian social democratic movement. That's one of the reasons for the relatively more progressive character of Canadian politics. People just left. People who were represented by Bob La Follette, the founder of the progressive movement, and others.

In fact, if you penetrate surface propaganda, I think people tend to accept these ideas. You can see it, for example, in polls about almost any issue you look at, say, medical care. There has been enormous corporate propaganda to try to demonize the idea of some form of national health care. But if you look at polls going far back, when people are asked, "Is health a right that the government should defend?" you get very high support. In fact, in the Reagan years, one of the questions that the Gallup poll asked was, "Do you think there ought to be a constitutional amendment that guarantees the right to health care?" About 70 percent of the population agreed. In fact, about 40 percent of the population thought there already was such a constitutional amendment because it's so obviously right.

If you take a look at referenda over the years, they start with enormous support for national health care. Then the corporate propaganda starts—you won't be able to see your doctor, you will lose your health care, the government's going to take everything from you, it goes on and on—and you see the numbers supporting it drop.

We're seeing that right now, in fact. The popular support is the right below the surface on major issues. It gets beaten down by scare tactics.

But you have to penetrate the surface of doctrine and propaganda and ideology. I think when you do, you find a lot of common humanity, lots of ways for people to overcome the divisiveness that seems to plague them on the surface.

People are asking if Trump can be beaten in the 2020 election, and who could do it.

Your guess is as good as mine. I don't have any crystal ball. I think it's touch and go. It depends on popular mobilization, dedication, commitment, breaking through the flood of lies and distortions.

I should mention something that we all know but don't talk about. The crucial issues that really matter for our lives and for our children's lives and future generations are not even being discussed in the election campaign. Not discussed.

The worst policies, the worst crimes of the Trump administration—there are lots of crimes, but the worst ones, far and away beyond any others, are climate policy and nuclear weapons policy. Those just swamp everything else in significance. Is anybody talking about them on the campaign trail? Are they an issue in the impeachment proceedings? The really critical topics are off the agenda.

If you ask whether Trump can be defeated, one of the ways would be to put those issues right in the center of political concern. Everybody, except somebody who is really a pathological maniac, wants their grandchildren to have a decent life. Nobody wants their grandchildren to hate them as the worst criminals in history, which is what's going to happen the way things are going.

Who wants that, just to put a few more dollars in your pocket? Not many people, I don't think. I think people can be reached on that.

Let me ask you about something called PEP. Progressive Except Palestine. It's kind of an interesting aspect of our scene in this country that many people advocate the rule of law, promote human rights, extol the principle of self-determination, and call for freedom and justice everywhere, except for Palestine. That issue has been so central to your political activism and commitment over the years, and Palestine is still under occupation.

Worse than that. Gaza, which is the most horrendous victim, is probably going to become literally uninhabitable within a few years. Gaza is under constant Israeli attack, boycott, the closing of borders, the closing of opportunities, the destruction of the health system, the power system, the sanitation system, preventing fishermen from going out more than a couple miles, constant military attacks, slaughter, and destruction. The United Nations monitors are literally predicting that in a couple of years it will be uninhabitable.[20]

Meanwhile, the West Bank, the rest of the area, is being sliced up by settlement programs. This has been going on since about 1970 in one way or another. Both major political groupings are involved in a systematic plan designed to construct a kind of greater Israel, which includes what's called now Jerusalem, which is about five times the size of what it ever was before. Jerusalem took in lots of Palestinian villages, and now, under Trump's changing of US policy, has been authorized to be annexed by Israel. That's a sharp change.

To the east, there are corridors built which bisect what remains of the Palestinian territory, all Jewish towns, Ma'ale Adumim, Ariel, and others. It's all being integrated into Israel by very extensive infrastructure developments. If any of you happen to have visited, you know that you can travel around the West Bank on superhighways and not even know that there is a Palestinian in existence. These are all Jewish-only or tourist-only road structures. Meanwhile, the areas of Palestinian population concentration are being avoided and encircled. Like the heavy population, say, in Nablus, don't touch that.

The idea is to create a system that, when it all gets integrated and annexed into Israel, won't affect what they call "the demographic problem." The demographic problem means too many non-Jews in a Jewish state. It won't affect that because the Palestinian populations are either being avoided or they're being expelled. In the Jordan Valley, it's largely being expelled, which is a real dense takeover. By now, I think there are about 160 or so Palestinian enclaves, which are pretty much separated from one another. Farmers are separated from their fields and so on. A very systematic policy.

That's what's been developing before our eyes for pretty much fifty years. The United States has been supporting it with enormous aid.

How about the population here? What do they think about it? I think that's pretty interesting. It used to be an untouchable issue. For years, I've tried to give talks on this. I literally had to have police protection at universities. I would go to a major university—take one case, UCLA. Back in the 1980s, I spent a week giving philosophy lectures, but I was also giving political talks, as I usually do. Most of them were on Central America at that time. But one professor, a guy who actually happened to be teaching half the year in Tel Aviv, asked me to give a talk on the Middle East. I said, "Of course, glad to."

The next day, I got a phone call from the campus police saying they wanted me to have uniformed police with me the entire time I was on campus. I didn't accept that, so they had undercover police following me around the whole time, sitting in on philosophy lectures. The talk itself was under airport security: one entrance, inspecting handbags, and so on. There were meetings physically broken up, even at my own university, MIT. It was almost impossible to talk about Israel/Palestine. Nobody complained at that time about free speech or anything. This was fine.

About fifteen or twenty years ago, it started to change. It's now radically different. You go to give a talk on Israel/Palestine, you can barely get a hostile question. It's not necessarily a good thing, because these are issues that should be thought about. But there's a radical change.

It shows up even in polls. For example, the base for support for Israeli policies used to be in liberal circles. The Democrats were the main source for support for Israeli policies. That's radically changed. Now a majority of people who identify themselves as liberal Democrats are more supportive of Palestinians. This is especially true among young people. Support for Israel in the United States has moved over to the far right: evangelical Christians, ultranationalists, part of the Republican Party.

This offers real opportunities for changes in US policy. Unfortunately, it's not being pressed by solidarity movements. I think this should be their top priority, getting US policy to change. Looking at the public attitudes and looking at the actual policies, I don't think that's impossible.

You should bear in mind that US military aid, probably all aid to Israel, is illegal under US law. That's a point that could be pressed and made public. Why is it illegal? For one thing, because of the Symington Amendment of 1976, which bans US aid, particularly military aid, to any country that constructs nuclear weapons and does not accept the Non-Proliferation Treaty.

Israel, of course, has a huge nuclear arsenal. The way the United States gets around it is by pretending it doesn't know that Israel has nuclear weapons. Of course, everybody knows it does. It's a perfectly open secret. But they pretend—we don't know, maybe they do, maybe they don't—so we can keep military aid pouring in. Obama had this huge flood of military aid, $30 billion over ten years or something like that, by pretending that they don't know that Israel has nuclear weapons.

There is also the Leahy Law, named after Senator Patrick Leahy, which ban military aid to any military unit that is engaged in systematic human rights violations. The human rights violations are so extreme that we don't even have to talk about them. I think those are issues that could be pressed.

What would constitute justice for the Palestinians? What do they want?

For a long time, what the Palestinians wanted—and what majority opinion was in favor of—was a Palestinian state alongside Israel.

The two-state solution.

The two-state solution. That is, again, not talked about here. But if you go back to the early 1970s, that became a major issue on the international agenda. In 1976, a resolution was introduced in the UN Security Council that was supported by the major Arab states, Egypt, Syria, and Jordan. It called for a two-state settlement on the internationally recognized border, with guarantees for the right of each state to exist in peace and security within secure and recognized borders. Israel was infuriated. They refused to attend the session. The United States vetoed it and continued to veto similar resolutions in later years.

You could argue that the border should be adjusted. It's a military demarcation line, so maybe you could straighten it out or something. But that was a possible solution, supported by a majority of Palestinians for a long time.

By now, many Palestinians, probably most, have given up hope on that. They say it's just impossible. The settlement has reached such a level that it can't be done.

Personally, I don't agree with that. I think it's still in the ballpark if US policy shifts. But that leaves them without an option. Many Palestinians, including Palestinian intellectuals, talk about what they call a one-state solution. There should be one-state from the Jordan to the Mediterranean with equal rights for everyone. That's simply not an option. You can talk about it.

Because?

For a very simple reason. First of all, it has zero international support. It's not going to be supported by African states, for example. States are very jealous of their sovereignty. And notice that a one-state solution means Israel goes out of existence.

As a Jewish state.

As it is now constituted. It's not going to be Israel anymore. It's going to be a majority Palestinian state, whatever you call it. There is no support for that anywhere.

Furthermore, if there were any support, Israel would use every weapon at its command, including its huge nuclear arsenal, to prevent it. It's kind of academic, because there is no support for it. So, putting your hope in that is totally meaningless.

In fact, the choices today, and for several years, have been between the two-state settlement and some sort of greater Israel with Palestinians essentially tossed away.

You could argue—and it has been argued—that there could be some kind of one-state settlement that maintains Jewish sovereignty but allows some kind of role for Palestinians, a kind of mildly apartheid state. Not pretty, but maybe that could happen.

What's your position on boycott, divestment, and sanctions? Are you in favor or against?

First of all, it's boycott and divestment. There are no sanctions. That's just a slogan.

BDS.

BDS is a slogan, but the reality is BD, so let's be honest about it. Sanctions only come from the United States, and they're not coming. So, what about boycott and divestment? I think those are good tactics. But you have to think when you carry out tactics. You can't just say, "I have a catechism and I'm going to apply it." You have to ask, "How am I going to apply it?"

If you take a look back, the boycott and divestment initiatives began in 1997 with an Israeli left activist, Uri Avnery. He and his peace group, Gush Shalom, organized a boycott and divestment campaign aimed at Israel's occupation of the occupied territories. That made very good sense. That's a clear issue. There was plenty of support for it, no way of opposing it, and it strikes right at the heart of the major issues. And there have been successes in that. For example, the Presbyterian Church, a big organization, not only has a boycott and divestment program against the settlements but also against US multinationals that are involved in any way in the settlements. That's exactly the right program. That kind of thing has been successful.

Most of that has been done outside the BDS movement. They have a catechism, three points: one point is the occupation; the second point is all Palestinian refugees must have the right of return to Israel; third, we have to boycott Israel until it provides equal rights for Palestinians. You can argue about whether those latter two goals are right or wrong, but one thing is very clear about them. They're not going to be realized, and they are going to engender a reaction which is stronger than the protest. They're going to engender cries of anti-Semitism and academic freedom, diverting attention away from the Palestinians to some extraneous issue, legislation to ban BDS because it's anti-Semitic, why Israel and not a dozen other countries? and so on.

It's going to be condemned as utterly hypocritical. If you boycott Tel Aviv University, why not boycott Harvard? The United States has a far worse record than Israel does.

Aside from being unprincipled, the goals are unrealizable, and their main effect is to divert attention away from the plight of Palestinians to something else: freedom of speech, academic freedom, oppressive legislation. Everything but the plight of Palestinians. That's a very pointless choice of tactics.

The right tactics, I think, are apparent. They ought to be focused on the occupation and on US government policy, the kinds of things I mentioned, which can be changed. Even a credible threat of cutback of US aid would have an enormous effect. I think that those are pretty feasible goals. There are plenty of Americans across the board who, if they knew about it, wouldn't see any reason to provide military aid that happens to be in violation of US law. A lot of people would be opposed to that. It's also a way to bring up the major issues.

On the other hand, concentrating on, say, the right of return—first of all, it's never going to happen. Everybody knows it's never going to happen. And it diverts attention away from the real issues. The same with cultural boycotts. Maybe you can give an argument for them, but their effect in the real world is to divert attention away from the plight of Palestinians. That's the last thing you want in a solidarity movement.

So, I think while the BDS movement has great opportunities, I don't think it's realizing them because of the rigid structure of the doctrine that it accepts. And you just can't deal with the world that way. You can't have rigid doctrines that you try to apply, whatever the human consequences. You're never going to get anywhere that way, in personal life or anything else.

But you do see cracks in what you described as a monolithic support for Israel.

Oh, plenty.

On Tuesday, August 20, at 8:00 a.m., the FBI came to my door. Agents Carlos Medina and Brian Palmer wanted to know about my trip to Iran and whether I knew certain people. They wanted me to "share" my experiences in Iran. "We're interested in your story," they said, "because the Iranian government targets people to manipulate."

I said very little, and I told them to just leave. And they did leave after about ten minutes. But it was enough to scare my wife, Kadriye, who is from Turkey and has some experience with state authorities knocking on doors or breaking doors down.

As someone who has spent a lifetime in dissent and confronting state power and its depredations, I know you've had some experiences with what the late John Trudell called the Federal Bureau of Intimidation.

I've had experiences, but some of them are kind of funny. So, for example, take the Pentagon Papers. I was a friend of Dan Ellsberg's, and I had advance copies of the Pentagon Papers. I was one of the people helping to distribute them while he was underground. I was getting phone calls from newspapers in the United States and Europe and elsewhere asking if they could get a part of the Pentagon Papers. They didn't have any trouble finding me. The FBI never found me, literally. They did come to my door, but only after Dan surfaced and identified himself. I wouldn't talk to them.

The incompetence of the intelligence agencies is pretty astonishing. One of the reasons is, they're always looking for people like themselves. For example, during some of the trials of the resistance, the FBI was never able to find out what was being done because they were always asking, "Where are the orders coming from? Are they coming from North Korea? Hungary?" It couldn't be that Americans are standing up in town hall in New York and saying, "We hereby conspire to undermine the Selective Service System." Don't pay attention to that. That's enough to put them all in jail, but we're not going to look at that, because that's obviously a cover for something, so let's find out what's really going on.

That's what was going on. Nothing else. It's one of the ways to outfox intelligence services.

You're turning 91 on December 7.

So they claim.

As you move forward, what do you have up your sleeve?

I'm not going to tell you. At 97, maybe I'll tell you. [*laughs*]

At 97, we'll be back, hopefully. Thank you very much, Noam.

THE POLITICS OF THE PANDEMIC

Oro Valley, Arizona   May 5, 2020

Some years ago you wrote, "Among the hardest tasks that anyone can undertake, and one of the most important, is to look honestly in the mirror. If we allow ourselves to do so, we should have little difficulty in finding the characteristics of 'failed states' right at home."[1] What does the current coronavirus pandemic reveal about characteristics of the United States as a failed state?

Fifteen years ago, I wrote a book called *Failed States*. It was mostly about the United States, a country that is a danger to its own citizens and to the world, violates international law, fails to develop internal systems that sustain its own people, and much else. It's much more extreme today. By now I think it's a widely held opinion about the United States, abroad and at home.

I just happen to have read a Canadian newspaper this morning, the *National Observer*. One of the main articles in it is "Have Americans Gone Crazy?"[2] George Packer, kind of a mainstream liberal intellectual, recently wrote an article called "We Are Living in a Failed State."[3]

Now, take a look at the coronavirus. Countries have responded to it in different ways. Right now, there is an epidemic of China bashing, mostly an effort to try to cover up Trump's crimes against the American people and to find some scapegoat. The facts of the

61

matter are that by January 12, a few days after the first discovery that something was going on, Chinese scientists had identified the virus, sequenced the genome, and given the information to the World Health Organization and to the entire world. So, by January 12, every relevant scientist all over the world knew what was happening and what to do about it.

And then after that, countries varied. The countries of Asia and Oceania—Australia, New Zealand, Taiwan, South Korea—reacted quite quickly and very effectively. They have coronavirus pretty much under control by now, close to eradication in some places. Europe didn't pay a lot of attention to these Asians at first, but most countries gradually got their act together more or less in varying ways, some pretty well, some not.

Way at the bottom of the barrel is the United States. US intelligence was battering at the doors of the White House, issuing daily reports, trying to get somebody's attention. The top health officials were trying to do the same. Trump wouldn't listen. He has surrounded himself with a bunch of sycophants who, if they understand anything, wouldn't dare say anything to the lord. He apparently, from all reports, has two interests: TV ratings and the stock market. The stock market doesn't have much to do with the economy, but in his fantasy world, it tells him whether he's going to be elected in November.

So, the stock market finally tanked in March. He noticed, so he made some statements. Meanwhile, tens of thousands of Americans had already died. The pandemic was raging, totally out of control. After that comes a series of—if it weren't so tragic, you would call them comedy acts. One day, it's nothing, it's like a bad cold, I've got it totally under control. The next day, it's a pandemic and I was the first person to notice it, before anyone else did. The next day, a lockdown. The next day, open up by Easter. On and on.

But there is one theme that runs through: I've got to make sure that I'm on top. It doesn't matter what happens to anyone else. If the scientist in charge of vaccines happens to say something criticizing some of my quack medicine proposals, I'll fire him. He's fired. So we lost the head of vaccines.[4]

If, during my anti-China tirades, a major operation working with Chinese scientists is discovering new coronaviruses and working on ways of protecting against them, but it happens to have some contact with Chinese scientists, destroy the program.[5] That's the way we are. If it turns out to be convenient to denounce the World Health Organization and score some points with parts of my voting base who don't like international institutions and hate foreigners, okay, we'll defund the WHO and plan to destroy it.[6]

Of course, there are consequences, which, interestingly, don't get discussed. So, say, take Yemen, the worst humanitarian crisis in the world, for which Trump has his share of responsibility, along with his predecessor. There are health workers saving people there from the WHO, so, let's get them out and destroy it. Africa is suffering from many diseases. The WHO is on the frontline, saving people, but who cares? I could earn some points with my voting base, so let's kill a lot of Africans. That's typical.

In fact, if you want to get kind of an encapsulated view of the thinking of Trump and the people around him, probably the best place to look for a brief picture is his budget proposal for next year. It came out on February 10, right in the middle of the pandemic, though he was still calling it a cold.

So what's in the budget? Well, there is a decrease in funding in some areas, an increase in funding in others.[7] Let's take a look. What about health areas? The Centers for Disease Control and Prevention, cut 9 percent. Actually, Trump has been systematically defunding the CDC every year since he's been in office. In the midst of the pandemic, let's defund it further. In fact, anything health-related or anything that's in service to the population, let's defund.

What about increases in funding? Increased subsidies to the fossil fuel industries hard at work to ensure that organized human society won't exist in another couple generations. So, fund them. It's great for profits. It's my constituency—wealth and corporate power. So, fund them, whatever the consequences—and defund others that just serve people and save lives.

That's what we're dealing with. That's the malignancy that happens to be running the country and the political sector.

In terms of your perspective on US history, has there ever been a time when there has been such disdain for science as exists in the current regime in Washington?

Never. There's never been anything remotely like it. There wasn't much interest in science for a long time, but what there was took science seriously. This is off the spectrum.

And it's not just the United States. The great writer Ariel Dorfman recently quoted a fascist general under Francisco Franco back in 1936 in Spain, General Millán-Astray. He said, "Down with intelligence! Long live death!"[8] That's Trump and the guys around him: down with intelligence, forward with death.

Not him alone. Trump's favorite friend in South America, Jair Bolsonaro in Brazil, is exactly the same. There are others around the world: his favorite dictator, Abdel Fattah el-Sisi in Egypt; Mohammed bin Salman, the killer leader of Saudi Arabia; Narendra Modi in India.

Some of it is grotesque, like the Environmental Protection Agency, which is now a subsidiary of the coal lobby. The scientists there are almost totally silenced.

Let's take a look at the last person that Trump awarded a Medal of Freedom to, Rush Limbaugh, one of the chief sources of information for Republicans and one of the people Trump listens to all the time. So, what does he say? He says there are four corners of deceit: media, government, academia, and science. They exist on the basis of deceit. They're committed to deceit. So, throw them out. Down with intelligence, long live death. That's the slogan.

Take a look at what has happened to the health system. Hospitals have to be run on a business model. What's the model? No spare capacity, even at the best hospitals in the world. You don't want to waste resources. So not an extra hospital bed.

Who wants that? It doesn't work very well, even when the system is working. Plenty of us can attest to that. I can, too. But if anything goes wrong, tough luck.

Other countries, which were also committed to the neoliberal monstrosities, didn't go anywhere near this far. We're an unusually business-run society. Take Germany, the most successful state capitalist country in the world. Germany is very committed to austerity and neoliberalism—or *ordoliberalism*, as they call it. But they didn't destroy the hospital system. They had spare beds, spare diagnostic capacity. When the pandemic struck, they could get things in order, and it was pretty well controlled, with quite a low death rate.

Not in the United States. Here it's going out of control, and it's going to get worse. If you stop the lockdown, put people out in the streets to converge. What Trump and the guys around him are obviously hoping is that they can somehow make it look as though the economy is recovering in time for the election. If a lot of people die, to hell with it.

First of all, the people dying are mostly poor people, Black people, and people without privilege. They're the ones who suffer worst. So, you can start propaganda about these people. You can blame it on them and say it's the cities, the centers of rot and immigrants and Puerto Ricans and all those bad people. That's the propaganda line. If a couple hundred thousand people die, as Bolsonaro put it recently when confronted with the rising deaths in Brazil thanks to his policies, he said, "So what?"[9]

That's the thinking in this kind of protofascist mentality and the social patterns that are developing. I wouldn't call it fascism. It gives it too much credit to call it fascism. Fascism had an ideology, a horrible one, but at least an ideology. Here it's nothing but benefiting myself, the rich around me, and so on.

That's probably Trump's tactic for the coming election. It will be terrible for the population. It may give a superficial impression of something working, if he can carry it off. Who knows? It depends on whether the population will let him get away with it.

You mentioned the Great Depression. You have memories of bread lines and soup kitchens. Today there are car lines for miles and miles, people trying to get some free food. Food banks and charities are stretched thin. You alluded to political differences in the country. This economic crisis, was triggered by a health catastrophe, the pandemic, and that's a fundamental difference between what's going on today and what happened in the 1930s.

It's different but there are some similarities. The 1920s were very much like the neoliberal period. The labor movement was crushed. Woodrow Wilson's Red Scare was the final blow. There had been a very vibrant, vital labor movement. It was crushed by force. In the 1920s, it was gone.

The financial institutions were roaring, going out of sight. All sorts of scams were going on, unbelievable ones. My father, for example, who was an immigrant and didn't know that much about what was going on, bought some land in Florida. He was convinced it would be a great deal. It turned out that his "land" was out in the middle of the Atlantic Ocean somewhere.

I never told you this, but my father, who was an immigrant and didn't speak much English, bought some land on Long Island— this was in the 1920s—and when he went out there, he found there were twenty other people also holding a deed to the same property.

That happened to one of my relatives, too, in upstate New York.

That's the kind of stuff that was going on. Huge wealth accumulating, financial manipulations. Pretty much like the neoliberal period in many ways.

As a society, the United States has been collapsing through the whole neoliberal period. Infrastructure is collapsing. You can't drive on the roads, bridges are crumbling, hospitals are failing. And the economy has been taken over by financial institutions. The huge growth of financial institutions is one of the main developments during the neoliberal period. They do almost nothing for the economy—and probably harm it.

It starts with Reagan. Remember, one of the first things that he did, almost on his first day in office, was to try to smash the labor unions.

The air traffic controllers.

Yes, and opening the door to using scabs, which then Caterpillar and corporations picked up. It's very important to destroy the labor unions. They might lead to progress for the general population, as they did in the 1930s. So that's understandable.

But Reagan did more. He was really working hard for his bosses, corporate power. One of his first acts was to legalize tax havens and stock buybacks. It kind of sounds arcane. It's not. That's trillions of dollars stolen from the public. Tax havens amount to tens of trillions of dollars. Apple sets up a room in Ireland and says, this is where we are, we don't have to pay higher taxes elsewhere. That means you pay taxes, I pay taxes.

Stock buybacks are an enormous way of enriching management, CEOs, and rich shareholders, meanwhile undermining the actual enterprise. We're seeing that right before our eyes now. Take the airline industry running cap in hand to the nanny state, saying, "Please bail us out. We need $50 billion." Why do they need $50 billion? In the mad rush to enrich yourself, gorging at the pigsty. After the 2008 crisis, airlines were enriching themselves with stock buybacks, roughly about $50 billion worth, certainly not improving the operation of the airlines. Anybody who has taken a trip on the airlines knows that. Not building the industry, just enriching themselves. That's happening all over the corporate sector.

That was illegal before Reagan, and the laws were enforced. The Treasury Department actually worked. It enforced the ban on tax havens and stock buybacks.

So, yes, it was a failed society before the pandemic hit.

In fact, why do we have a pandemic altogether? In 2003, after the SARS epidemic, which was a coronavirus, scientists understood very well—and, in fact, told us—there's going to be another coronavirus pandemic. We know how to deal with it. We can prepare. Just like they're telling us now, we prepare for the next pandemic.

But somebody has to do something about it. Who is going to do something about it? The drug companies are ruled out. They're bloated with wealth. The public gives them massive subsidies. Wealth is coming out of their ears. They have all the resources, the scientists, everything else. But they can't do anything because of something called capitalism. They're supposed to follow market signals. You listen to Milton Friedman. You're just supposed to enrich yourselves. So, they can't do anything. There's no profit to be made from fending off a disaster that's going to come in ten years.

The government could easily step in, the National Institutes of Health—great scientists, plenty of resources—along with the Centers for Disease Control, and many others. But that's blocked. That's the neoliberal disaster. Government is the problem. So, nobody can do it.

Obama made a few minor efforts, but they were blocked by neoliberal savagery. Meanwhile, Trump came along and started making it much worse, defunding the Centers for Disease Control and others, canceling programs that were working to try to detect problems, working in China with Chinese scientists to try to find out where possible problems might come from. All of that gets the axe. Why? You don't enrich your constituency that way.

Trump's constituency is great wealth, corporate power. He doesn't give a damn about anyone else. There's some faking with populist rhetoric, and maybe some people believe it. But just look at the entire legislative program. Nobody matters except the rich and powerful and the corporate sector, the rich business sector.

So, everything gets wiped out. You're uniquely vulnerable. Then come along the catastrophes I've been talking about since. The society was already in deep trouble. First of all, there were huge amounts of debt—corporate debt, private debt. People were in debt because wages had stagnated. Meanwhile the cost of living goes up. People are driving cars to pick up food. In the 1930s, they weren't driving cars. My father couldn't get a secondhand car until the New Deal in 1937.

It's a much richer society, which means it should be much easier, if the society were functioning, to deal with this problem. But when you're catering to 0.1 percent and the rest don't matter—that's a little bit of an exaggeration: the top 10 percent or 15 percent, they matter too, not like the 0.1 percent, of course—if that's the way society works, you're going to be in deep trouble.

But doesn't the 0.1 percent need to keep the patient alive? If everybody is destitute and penurious, they won't be able to buy the products that the system produces.

I'm sure you saw, about a year ago, a group of top CEOs issued a manifesto saying, we've done bad things.[10] We realize it. But now we're changing. From now on, we're going to be dedicated to the welfare of you guys. The peasants with the pitchforks are coming at us. We're going to be devoted to you. Don't worry—it's all under control.

This got even more dramatic at the Davos meetings last January. As you know, every January the rich and powerful converge on a ski resort in Switzerland.

The "masters of mankind."

The masters of mankind. They all get together, they go skiing, they have parties, they congratulate each other on how wonderful they are. This last Davos meeting was different. There was a theme running through it very much like those 181 executives: We've made mistakes, we recognize them. From now on, we're going to be different. We're going to be working for ordinary people, you guys, the peasants with the pitchforks. Just leave it to us. We've got it under control.

People who can remember the 1950s—I'm old enough—can remember that the same thing happened then. At that time, it was called the "soulful corporation." Corporations are not just in it for themselves, their rich shareholders, their CEOs, their management. They are in it for everybody. They are soulful, they work for the public.

We've had a number of years to notice how soulful they are.

This is, incidentally, liberals that I'm quoting—the people who then went on to the Kennedy administration—not from the right. And they probably meant it. I'm not saying they were deceitful. They probably meant, yes, that's what corporations ought to be. There's such a thing as capitalism in the background, but we somehow don't want to think about that. And it wasn't yet in its savage era, the neoliberal era that began pretty much with the Reagan years, slightly before.

So, we're now reenacting this. We're concerned. Something has to be done for the public. How much? Well, as little as we can get away with.

You follow the scientific journals and reports. What have you learned about this coronavirus? What can we expect? There are wild estimates about how many people are going to die or how many people are going to be infected. What do people need to know?

You have to look at those estimates carefully. For one thing, they all have a wide margin of error because a lot is just not understood.

Actually, much more could have been understood if somebody had started serious research on coronaviruses. There are a lot of them, most of them perfectly harmless, some serious. It could have been understood if Trump hadn't killed the programs working in China with Chinese scientists.

But because of all these crimes, not too much is known about coronaviruses.

Furthermore, you have to be careful not to fall for the right-wing propaganda. So, when the Imperial College in London says 510,000 will die in the United Kingdom, and maybe 2.2 million in the United States, and a couple of months later it says, maybe 50,000 in England, you turn on Fox News and they say the scientists are just a deceitful gang of people who don't know anything.[11]

Actually, they know exactly what they're doing. When you look at those two estimates, both were quite plausible. The first was on the assumption that the government would continue with the program that Prime Minister Boris Johnson had initiated, namely, do nothing. Later, when Britain joined Europe and started to institute significant lockdown programs, other programs to test and so on, the same estimates came out much lower. But they're plausible in both cases under different conditions, and still with a wide margin of error because they just don't know much.

One thing is pretty clear. There is a very close statistical correlation between imposing lockdowns and controlling and containing the disease. Actually, the countries that started early, like, say, South Korea, didn't even have to go to lockdowns. They were doing massive testing and tracing, which is the right way to do it. You test people. If you find somebody with the symptoms of the virus, isolate them, find out who their contacts were, isolate those people, and let the mass of the population who hasn't been infected continue.

You can do that in the early stages. When you let it get to the US stage, thanks to Trump and his guys, it's hopeless. First of all, we're still not testing. The testing is ridiculously low. It's gotten so far out of hand that you can't do the serious tests and trace measures. So, the only method is to keep the lockdown. You can try to relax it slightly here and there, taking account of circumstances.

But to do what, say, the governors of Florida and Georgia are doing or what the demonstrators in Michigan are calling for, is just to ask for disaster.

Deborah Birx, one of the government scientists on the coronavirus task force, calls the abandoning of mitigation efforts, the spacing and distancing, "devastatingly worrisome."[12]

You will notice that when Birx, Anthony Fauci, or any other scientist is around, they're very cautious so as not to step on the toes of the megalomaniac fanatic who is running the show. Everyone has to be very cautious in what they say, because you can't offend the dear leader. If you say anything that offends Trump, you're out. If they were talking freely, they would be much more open— you can be certain about that.

We've recently passed the fiftieth anniversary of Earth Day, and we're in a major ecological crisis today. Dr. Stephen Bezruchka points out that the loss of habitat and deforestation have brought the animal kingdom in much closer contact with humankind, and that has caused a growth in coronaviruses.[13]

That's exactly what happened in China. But it's quite general. As habitat is destroyed, animals that humans have had no contact with come out of the forests, and humans move in. There's more contact. One of the most serious cases is bats. They happen to have massive amounts of coronaviruses. That's why very courageous Chinese scientists have been venturing into dangerous places, deep inside caves and so on—and many died—to try to collect information about the coronaviruses. They found a ton of information. US scientists were working with them for some time, until the cooperation was canceled by the killer in the White House.

As it expands, high-tech agriculture, which is in itself unsustainable, is destroying the topsoil. We won't have topsoil in a couple of generations, if you continue with unsustainable industrial agribusiness, destroying habitat. If you open up the national parks to fossil fuel companies—another one of Trump's crimes— it's kind of a double whammy. One thing is it increases the use of fossil fuels, to which he's dedicated, his passionate desire to destroy the possibility for human life in the short term. And that's not an exaggeration. He knows exactly what he's doing. He just doesn't give a damn.

What's going to happen? The spread of more diseases. Maybe coronavirus, maybe something else.

In many ways, we're acting to destroy not only ourselves but life on Earth. Let's not forget that the Anthropocene, as we're now calling it, the period since World War II—the geological epoch of humans having a massive and destructive impact on the global environment—is a period of not only global warming, which is bad enough and escalating, but also destruction of habitats: plastics destroying ocean life, uncontrolled trash and sewage, unsustainable agriculture, and industrial meat production. And the incredibly reckless use of antibiotics means that bacteria mutate much more quickly, so now there are bacteria for which there are no remedies.

All of these actions, driven by the need for more profit and more power, are causing massive destruction of species. We're right in the middle of what's called the Sixth Extinction. The Fifth Extinction was 65 million years ago, when a huge asteroid hit Earth and killed most of life on the planet. We're doing the same. We're in the Sixth Extinction. Not just humans. Insect populations are rapidly disappearing. In the places where they've been measured—it's pretty hard to measure—a majority of insect species are declining rapidly and some outright disappearing.[14] We survive on the basis of insects. So do many other species. It's just massive destruction.

This is all savage and cruel and is opening the door to pandemics.

Fortunately, there are ways out. Every one of the problems we're talking about—and many that we didn't—have solutions that are within reach. But you've got to do something about it. It's like the coronavirus pandemic. You can know how to deal with it, but that's no good unless somebody does something with the knowledge.

It's the same with every other one of these crises. The knowledge is there, the understanding is there—not entirely, but you can build on it. But somebody has to act.

If you're in the grips of a particularly savage form of state capitalism, neoliberal capitalism, what's amazingly called libertarianism in the United States, then you're toast. Nothing can be done. Corporations, obviously, aren't going to do it. Business can't do it.

There's a lot of concern today about the safety of the food chain, particularly when it comes to meat. In the slaughterhouses in Colorado, Iowa, Nebraska, and other states there are many workers who have contracted the coronavirus, and they're being forced back to work. I'm wondering if this is not a form of germ warfare.

It is, and it's advocated by the entire Republican Party. Let's take Senator Lindsey Graham, who is supposed to be one of the people who resembles a human being. His latest is legislation to try to force people back to work. If the boss tells them, "You've got to go, even if there is a coronavirus," and they don't, they lose their unemployment insurance. Graham says that's going to be changed "over our dead bodies."[15]

It's not just the meat-packers. There we can understand it on the basis of pure racism. The meat-packers are mostly poor, Hispanic, Black.

We're also doing exactly the same thing across the border. Mexico wants to keep the factories, the maquiladoras, closed. The Trump administration says, you've got to open them, even if you die from coronavirus.[16] Our car manufacturers need leather seats. We don't care whether you die. This is pure savagery.

Juan González, an independent journalist, cohost of *Democracy Now!*, says, "I don't think we should discount the possibility that

this president will declare an election that he loses as a fraud and illegitimate, and attempt to stay in power."[17] How do you see the upcoming campaign, if there is going to be a campaign, and election evolving?

That could happen. The person in office happens to be a psychopathic megalomaniac who is concerned with nothing but himself. I think it's psychologically impossible for him to say, "I lost," in anything.

Furthermore, let's keep in mind something else. I can't vouch for this—I'm not certain it's true—but there are credible reports that the state attorneys general, particularly in New York, have a raft of charges, serious ones, that he's liable to as soon as he loses presidential immunity.

He is trying to organize, very obviously, a mass of adoring worshipers loaded with guns, ready to fight for the guy they regard as their savior, who is stabbing them in the back constantly. A lot of unpleasant characters—a lot of white nationalists, racists, xenophobes, many types that the Republican Party has been trying to organize for some time—could be storming the White House just like they're storming the state capitals, funded by major corporations, just like what's happening in the state capitals now. A lot of this is astroturf, it's pretty clear.

He also has behind him the centers of power in private wealth and corporate power. He's their man. They don't want a possible move to social democratic policies, the kind that most of the public wants. Who knows how far they will go? We may be a "soulful corporation" up to a point, but not when our huge, monstrous wealth is at stake.

Rob Larson has written a book called *Bit Tyrants*, which you favorably reviewed.[18] He's very worried about the power that Google, Facebook, Amazon, Microsoft, and Apple, the big five, are accumulating and particularly the implications it has for privacy and surveillance concerns.

That's been going on for some time. It's what Shoshana Zuboff, a business professor at Harvard University, calls "surveillance capitalism."[19] Even before the pandemic, which is giving vast amounts of information to these major tech corporations and, of course, to the government, there were huge masses of information being collected about everybody.

So, if you drive a car, the car is picking up information about what you're doing, where you're going, everything else that's connected with your driving. That's going right to your insurance company. We're getting to the point where you might get a warning saying, "You went through a red light. You do that once more, and your insurance is going up." Or they figured out you like Chinese restaurants, and you will get a notice saying there is a Chinese restaurant half a mile ahead. That sounds not too bad. It is bad.

It's already at the point that there is experimentation—this actually started in Sweden; it's coming here now—with implanting chips in workers. The inducement is, if you have a chip, you can get a free Coke at the vending machine. But the chip also monitors what you're doing.

This is already happening in less intrusive ways. For example, UPS monitors their truck drivers. If they stop too long to go to the bathroom, they will get a demerit. If they back up when they shouldn't have, they will get a demerit. You get too many, your job is on the line. They claim that they've improved efficiency considerably this way—more deliveries, fewer people. Amazon works like that. At the Amazon workplaces, people are very tightly monitored. You take the wrong path between this spot and that spot, you will get an electronic notice.

The ideal we're moving toward is something like what you see in parts of China where there are cities that operate on what's called a social credit system. You get, I don't know, one thousand points or whatever it is, and you're under tight monitoring: cameras, facial identification, electronics. If you jaywalk, you lose credits. If you help an old lady across the street, you gain credits. Pretty soon, it all gets internalized, and you don't even notice it. It's like stopping at red lights. It's just the way the world is. You live under tight, constant monitoring.

If you think about it, even having a job is like that. You're under a form of totalitarianism that Stalin never dreamed of. Stalin didn't tell you when you were allowed to go to the bathroom, who you were allowed to talk to, what clothes you had to wear. That's your job for most of your waking hours.

People think having a job is a wonderful thing. Spending most of your waking life as a slave to a totalitarian boss is the best thing you can look forward to. That's a big change. And we've internalized this. Not everybody, of course. Human dignity is not that far below the surface. But the idea of surveillance capitalism is to get us to internalize this.

It's going to get worse as you move into what's called the internet of things. Your refrigerator has some electronic device so if you're driving home, you can get it to move something out of the freezer or something like that. These connected devices are all going to be collecting information about you. Everything you do will be monitored and shared with these big tech companies, the Big Brother who is collecting your data in some huge facility in Utah or somewhere.

None of this has to happen. First of all, the big tech companies could be broken up. They could be required to meet the same conditions, say, that newspapers have to meet. If you're libeled in a newspaper, you can bring a libel suit. If you're libeled on Facebook, you can't do a thing. Why should they have that privilege? Personally, I don't believe in libel suits, but if they exist, it should be the same for these tech platforms.

Incidentally, these are not the only corporations that should be potentially broken up. What about the fossil fuel corporations? Why should they even exist? Their role in the world is to keep us going for a while but then to ensure our destruction. So why not take them over, work to socialize them, put them under control of the workers, and have them move toward renewable energy?

Why do we have to have these big financial institutions that mostly harm the economy? Break them up. Let's go back to the days when banks were banks. It's not too utopian to say, let's go back to the pre-Reagan years. In the pre-Reagan years, banks were not involved in developing complex financial instruments to rob the public and lead to financial crises. They were banks. You put money into them. If they had extra money, they lent it to somebody who wanted to do something. It's not utopian to say let's go back to that.

But as soon as Reagan came in, the regulations started to be dismantled. Clinton made it much worse with the massive deregulation of the variety pushed by Robert Rubin and Larry Summers. Deregulating derivatives was just asking for disaster, which came.

We saw that very dramatically when the housing bubble collapsed in 2007, followed by the financial crisis as a result. There was congressional legislation, the Troubled Asset Relief Program bailout legislation. It had two parts: bail out the perpetrators, the banks whose scams and trickery had caused the crisis, the lending agencies, but also give help to the people who were their victims, the people who were tossed out of their homes when they were foreclosed. Which one did Obama pursue? The first, not the second. I think that's a large part of the reason why the population turned, not only against the Democratic Party but against institutions, against government, and fell right into the pocket of a con man and a demagogue like Trump.

What accounts for the attacks on the Post Office?

The Post Office is interesting. The Post Office is a very efficient organization that serves the general public all over the place—in rural communities, in cities. It's even a friendly place. You get to know your letter carrier. You go into the post office, you talk to the clerk. You meet friends there. It's a social institution that also provides very necessary services.

That's bad in a number of ways. For one thing, it's helping the wrong people, the majority. For another thing, it's giving people a bad idea. Something that you own—the government, if it's democratic—can work for you. That's a terrible idea. Remember Reagan reading his lines? Government is a problem. Hand it over to the private sector. We don't want people to believe that a government institution can do something for them.

That's why, incidentally, the Republicans have been working hard to destroy the Post Office for years. Congress has passed crazy rules that make it almost impossible for the Post Office to function, like prefunding of pensions for decades in advance. They're not able to charge decent rates, not able to provide services. The Post Office would be the obvious place, as it once was, for people to do banking. People aren't going to put in $10 million, but the kind of deposits that ordinary people have, you could manage at the local post office. You don't have to deal with the gougers and usury. The Post Office could be a place where you vote. It could be all sorts of things. But we have to destroy it.

And there is something in the background that I'm sure the rich and powerful are thinking about. We're supposed to revere the framers of the Constitution, these godlike creatures. And you have reactionary courts run by what are called originalists, meaning we've got to attend to every word and intention of the famous Founders.

The Founders had some things to say that the rich and powerful don't want you to hear, in particular about the Post Office. The Post Office is in the Constitution. What was it supposed to do? It was supposed to provide subsidies to the press to ensure that there would be a free and independent press.

A large majority of Post Office business in the early years was journals and newspapers, and at very cheap rates, intended as a public subsidy to help foster a free and independent press. You want to get the population to understand that? You want people to notice this is about the only country that doesn't have public broadcasting? We have a tiny fringe, which is corporate run, but there's nothing like the BBC or French television.

Some public broadcasting, community radio and television, exists at the local level and is often very valuable. There could be a lot more of that if activists would make use of the opportunities.

There have been struggles about this all through modern history. We have to make sure that government does not serve the people. The worst possible thing imaginable is government of, by, and for the people. We have to kill any such idea. And we certainly don't want a free and independent press. So, the Post Office has to go.

I don't know how much Trump understands—probably not very much—but he understands enough to know that the Post Office serves people and not the very rich. They can use other means.

Say you're talking to a die-hard Bernie Sanders supporter who feels that their candidate was not treated well by the Democratic Party and says, "I'm going to sit this one out." What do you say to that person?

I would say three things. First of all, notice that the Sanders campaign has been an astonishing success in many ways. It's entirely shifted the arena of discussion, policy formation, and policy in too many ways to enumerate. And it hit the Democratic National Committee (DNC).

Take a look at the official Democratic Party program, what's now called Biden's program. It's way to the left of anything since FDR. Is it because the DNC suddenly had a conversion? No, it's because of the pressure from activists working, many of them under the Sanders umbrella, is working. That's one of many achievements.

The second thing to look at is why didn't Sanders get the nomination? It's true, the media were against him, the DNC were against him. But that's not the whole story. You have to look beyond that. Take a look at the primaries. Sanders was counting on an upsurge among younger voters, his supporters. Did it happen? No, it didn't happen. They didn't come out and vote. That's something to look at, especially if you're a Sanders supporter.

What else happened? Sanders didn't win two major constituencies: African Americans and women. If you look at their voting preferences, they preferred his policies but they didn't vote for him. And when you look at the studies that have been done, it seems the reason is they were saying to themselves, I like his policies but he's not going to be able to broaden the coalition to bring in so-called moderates, a broader group of people who will be able to get rid of Trump, which is the top priority.

Is that wrong? We don't know if that's wrong. In fact, if you look at the way Sanders fared in the Rust Belt, it may be right. That tells you something that has to be done. For activists who supported Sanders, we can reach out, not by abandoning our principles but by showing that they're the right principles for a much broader constituency, while not doing the kinds of things that might alienate them. We've got to work on that. So those are lessons.

The third point, which is about as complicated as 1+1=2, is that in this election, if it's going to be Biden or Trump—it doesn't matter in other states, but in swing states, you have two choices: one of them is to vote for Biden, the other is to not vote for Biden. To not vote for Biden takes a vote away from the opposition, which is the same as adding a vote for Trump. So, your two choices are vote against Trump or vote for Trump. That's basically what it comes down to. As I say, that's about as hard to figure out as 1+1=2. That's the choice.

Meanwhile, recognize what the left has always understood. Elections are a blip. They're a brief moment taken away from activism. The standard doctrine that the rich and powerful and the ruling groups want to drill into your head is that politics consists of voting once every four years. Then go home, and leave it to your betters. In fact, that's called progressive democratic theory. That's the official doctrine. Don't fall for it.

The correct doctrine is the left doctrine. What counts in politics is your constant, day-to-day activist work, the kind of things that change the social conditions, the understanding, the background conditions under which changes can happen. Every couple of years, an event comes along that would take you maybe fifteen minutes to think about. Take a look at the political system. Decide if there is a meaningful choice. If there is, take a couple minutes and go into the voting booth and vote against the worst guy. Because it can make a difference—in fact, a big difference.

Then go back to your activist work. Your activist work might be preparing for a campaign, like working in the Sanders campaign, which had a major effect. Or it can be other things. But that's the way you should look at elections, until the point when you actually move toward a party committed to being a government that's of, by, and for the people.

The Roosevelt administration had plenty of flaws, but it moved very far in that direction. It was a sympathetic administration, under tremendous popular pressure from the labor movement, political parties, activist groups. And it accomplished quite a lot, including Social Security, and made a big difference for years to follow.

So those are the choices for a supporter of Sanders. The worst choice is to say, "I didn't get what I wanted. I'm going to go home and sulk and let the world go to pot." That's the worst choice. That's giving the election to Trump.

While there is selfishness, people are also making tremendous sacrifices. I'm thinking of the doctors, nurses, emergency medical technicians, and caregivers who have done extraordinary work during the pandemic.

It's incredible. They're a real indication of what the human spirit can achieve. And the same is much more broadly true. Around the world—Brazil, here, other countries, often in the poorest communities—people are coming together in mutual support groups.

Let's join together to help that elderly guy who's stuck in his house somewhere and doesn't have any food. Or let's go organize a food bank. People are capable of all sorts of things.

On the international level, there's also an example of a country that's showing what genuine internationalism is. There's something called the European Union. There is a rich country, Germany, which has pretty much handled things for itself. A couple of miles to the south is a country called Italy, which is in trouble. Northern Italy has a serious pandemic. Is Germany helping them? No. But some country is. It's called Cuba, the country that we've had under our boot for sixty years, trying to crush it.

Cuba is sending doctors to the front lines all over the world to compensate for what the rich and powerful aren't doing. It's not new. It's been happening for a long time. But we're not allowed to notice that. That's the wrong message, like noticing that the Post Office works. But we could learn something from the Cubans.

How are you doing?

There are nuisances, but we're the lucky ones. Valéria and I are pretty naturally hermits. We're in a place where we can easily isolate. We have some space outside, and the Arizona desert is pretty empty. So, we're doing fine.

THE PRESIDENT, THE PANDEMIC, AND THE ELECTION

Oro Valley, Arizona   October 9, 2020

You were born in 1928, a decade after the misnamed Spanish flu hit the world, causing hundreds of thousands of deaths in the United States and many millions of deaths around the globe. I say misnamed because the first reported case was at a US military base in Kansas in 1918. When you were growing up in Philadelphia, did people talk about it? Do you have any memory of it?

You're correct. It started in a military base in Kansas. US soldiers going to Europe spread it in Europe, and then it spread all over.

I was born ten years later, in 1928. I never heard a word about it. I learned about it later, in history books. Ten years later, it had essentially no residue in the United States. I never ran into anyone who talked about it.

Let's talk about the current pandemic, which has resulted in the deaths of now almost 215,000 here and millions of cases, numbers that are certain to go much higher. The regime in Washington has come under wide criticism, particularly from the scientific and medical communities. The *New England Journal of Medicine* called the regime's handling of the pandemic "dangerously incompetent."[1] It has "taken a crisis and turned it into a tragedy. . . . Instead of relying on expertise, the administration has turned to uninformed 'opinion leaders' and charlatans who obscure the truth and facilitate the promulgation of outright lies." *Scientific American* broke with 175 years of tradition by endorsing the Democratic candidate.[2] What is your sense of what's going on with the pandemic and Washington's response?

Basically, they don't care. It is pretty astonishing that the major US medical journal, the *New England Journal of Medicine*, which has been around for over two centuries, has taken a stand on an election for the first time in its history. *Scientific American* the same.

It's outrageous. In fact, if we look back at the record, it's even more outrageous. It's worth looking back at the record because we are facing the same situation again that we faced in 2003. We'd better understand how this pandemic came about if we hope to prevent the next one. And the next one could be much worse.

We've been kind of lucky so far. There have been coronaviruses that are highly contagious but not very lethal, like this one is, and ones that have been highly lethal but not very contagious, like Ebola. The next one, for all we know, might be highly contagious and highly lethal, and we might be back to something like the Black Death. It's very likely to come.

So, let's just go back for a minute and look at what happened with this one, and specifically, what happened with Donald Trump and the Republican Party. In 2003, the SARS epidemic coronavirus was contained, and scientists told us pretty much what they're saying now. It's very likely others will come. We have to be prepared for it. The way we have to be prepared for it is to study coronaviruses, work out possible vaccines, put in place response systems so that when it comes we will be ready to move.

Well, when Obama came into office, his first step was to ask his scientific advisers to prepare a pandemic preparation program. They came back with a detailed program. It was implemented. That lasted until Donald Trump came into office and dismantled the program.[3] Trump's major operative principle is to wreck. Anything that exists that I didn't create, destroy—and anything I did do is the greatest thing in history, as Sean Hannity will confirm.

What happened in January? In late December, China was finding pneumonia-like symptoms of unknown etiology and reported it to the World Health Organization. Very quickly, they discovered what it was. By January 10, Chinese scientists had identified the coronavirus, sequenced the genome, provided the information to the World Health Organization and the world. At that point, countries noticed that the United States was singularly unprepared because of Trump's malevolence. Nevertheless, it's a rich country with plenty of resources. It could have reacted. It didn't. In January, governments that cared about their citizens did react. Many of them had the situation pretty quickly under control.

Take the borders of China. South China is where the epidemic was the worst. It has an eight-hundred-mile-long border with Vietnam. No cases in Vietnam. For months there were no cases. Now there is a handful of cases, essentially nothing. They acted at once. The same was true in East Asia and Oceania quite generally. South Korea, Taiwan, Singapore, Thailand, Australia, New Zealand quickly acted. Very much under control. The same was true elsewhere: Africa, Senegal, almost nothing. Several other countries in Africa moved at once. Almost no cases. Europe waited, but finally got its act together. Most of Europe is more or less under control, not entirely. The Nordic countries, pretty much under control. Germany, pretty much under control. Even Italy, which had a very severe pandemic, is now pretty much under control. Britain was the worst. The United States is off the spectrum.

If you look at the cases and deaths around the world, there are three countries that are way at the top: the United States first, India second, Brazil third. Maybe this is a coincidence, but all three of them have autocratic rulers who are trying to crush democracy. I could go into the details, but those three are way at the top in both respects. Fourth, well behind them, is Russia, another country not known for vibrant democracy.

Trump's behavior since January has been almost as if it was designed to maximize the crimes. He's personally responsible for arguably hundreds of thousands of deaths, certainly many tens of thousands. You can see it step by step. It never stops. There was a government scientist in charge of vaccine development. He questioned some of Trump's quack medicines. Fired. The programs that were working with the Wuhan Institute of Virology, the main research center for coronaviruses, canceled. We have to blame China for Trump's malevolence, so we have to cancel programs that might help us.

The most recent example is an international consortium that's working on cooperation on vaccine development, which is obviously the way to proceed, and working in a limited way on distributional problems, trying to make sure that if there are vaccines, they won't be monopolized by the very rich but will go to the people who need them. Trump reacted to this by pulling out of the consortium just a couple of weeks ago.[4] We don't want to be part of an international effort that might help Americans and everyone else.

Meanwhile, there is an international UN conference on biodiversity that is critically relevant to pandemics. Species are being destroyed at a crazy rate. Areas where wildlife can be sequestered from human contact are being destroyed, setting up all the conditions for further spread of pandemics. The United States is not attending. We will not participate in an international conference on biodiversity. I don't think the press has even covered this. When I asked somebody to check, the only thing they found was two minutes on NPR.[5] Maybe there's more.

That's what's happening before our eyes. You cannot measure the malevolence. The *New England Journal of Medicine* is kind. They call it incompetence. It's not incompetence. We know exactly what's going on. The idea is maximize the prospects for my election, benefit my constituency of the rich and the corporate sector. Nothing else matters.

Take deregulation. Of course, deregulation is part of the race to destruction from environmental catastrophe, which happens to be much more important than the pandemic. So, deregulate to increase corporate profits, including fossil fuel profits. Meanwhile, destroy the environment in which human life might survive and also protect Americans.

When you deregulate, say, emissions, mercury going into streams, the chemicals that cause brain damage for children, you hurt Americans. Primarily you hurt those living near the most polluting industries. That's not me, that's not you. We can afford not to live in those places. But there are people who can't afford not to live there: African Americans, Hispanics, Puerto Ricans, poor people in general. They're stuck there. That's maximizing pollution. Pollution is already a deadly killer. When you add pollution to a respiratory epidemic, it's a major killer.

Incompetence isn't the right word for this.

You mentioned Bob Woodward, the celebrated *Washington Post* journalist of Watergate fame. What did you think of his decision in his book *Rage* not to release the information that Trump said COVID-19 "is a killer. . . . It is the plague."[6] He held on to that information for months and months.

He gave his reasons.[7] You can judge them. My own judgment is that it was quite improper.

Woodward said it wasn't verified. He wanted to make sure all the i's are dotted and the t's are crossed and so on. Okay, that's an argument if you're writing a book for the interests of the future. But here, hundreds of thousands of lives are at stake. My own feeling is that it's worth releasing the information, even if it's not totally verified, at that point.

What is your assessment of media coverage of the pandemic in general?

The media coverage should have been along the lines of what I just described. It wasn't. Most of what I just described you can read about only in medical journals or scientific journals. It should have been front and center, going way back to 2003, and emphasizing the fact that we are now in the same situation. Scientists are saying now exactly what they said then.

We are still in the grips of capitalist logic and savage neoliberalism. We are still in the hands of leadership of extreme malevolence.

The three worst, perhaps, are those I mentioned, Trump in the lead; his clone, Bolsonaro, in Brazil, the second largest country in the hemisphere; the world's largest democracy—or perhaps I should say former democracy—India, in the hands of Modi, a monster who is trying to destroy the relics of Indian democracy, meanwhile killing huge numbers of Indians, turning India into a Hindu national religious ethnocracy and crushing the rights of Muslims, destroying Kashmir.

These are the three leaders. No one is even close in cases and deaths. I should say this is slightly misleading, because I'm not counting deaths per capita. When you look at that, you get a slightly different picture. It's worth looking at. But these figures are very striking.

And the malevolence is striking. We are now in a situation where further pandemics are very likely, with habitat destruction even more likely, with heating the atmosphere even more likely. Future pandemics might be worse than this one, as I mentioned. We know what needs to be done. We don't have a lot of time to do it. The same impediments to dealing with this one still exist. It's within our reach to overcome them, but if we don't work in a dedicated, committed way, it will happen. This is the course we're on, just as we are on a course toward environmental destruction unless we sharply change direction.

What are you hearing about possible vaccines being developed to address coronavirus? Who will administer it, and how much it will cost? Will Big Pharma make a killing?

It's in our hands. There's no reason for Big Pharma to make a killing.

If you look at vaccines and pharmaceuticals generally, a lot of the major work is done by the government, either by the National Institutes of Health or by direct grants to the pharmaceutical corporations from the government. Well, there is actually a law on the books from 1980, the Bayh-Dole Act, which says that if the government has a substantial role in the development of pharmaceuticals, they should be offered to the public at a competitive price. That's on the books, and if it were properly observed, that would mean no Big Pharma profits on government-funded vaccines, and so on.

We are also strangled, I should say, by one of Clinton's great gifts to neoliberalism, the World Trade Organization (WTO) rules that provide extraordinary patent rights—what are called intellectual property rights—of a kind that never existed in the past and would have prevented the development of the United States and every other country if they had existed. They amount to massive monopoly pricing rights.

They're a bonanza for the pharmaceutical industry. The government pays for crucial parts of the development of some drug, then tells the pharmaceutical companies, You can make the profits from it and keep them forever. A large part of what's called the wealth of the corporate sector in the United States comes from these so-called Trade-Related Aspects of Intellectual Property Rights (TRIPS).

That's one of the main reasons that Apple is a $2 trillion corporation. The iPhones are produced in China, but the people making them get almost nothing. The Foxconn corporation in Taiwan makes some profit, but a large part of it comes back here to Apple because they have the patent on the designs, and so on.

We don't have to accept that either.

The pharmaceutical corporations say, We need these patents or there won't be innovation. There are much better means of innovation than pouring dollars into the hands of the pharmaceutical corporations. Many of them have been worked out. The economist who has done most of the work on this is Dean Baker. You can read the details in his free online book *Rigged*.[8] He makes a lot of sensible proposals about how to get rid of this monstrosity.

So, yes, as in every other case, there are ways to deal with these problems, but you have to move. You can't let the powerful just run things the way they want.

Now, on whether vaccines are likely to be developed, I have no expert knowledge. I just read the scientific journals and report what they say. Right now it looks as though China is in the lead in developing a vaccine that is being subjected to pretty widespread trials.

What ought to be done is international cooperation on development of a number of vaccines. There are many different approaches. We don't even know if any will work or which might work. They should be developed cooperatively, not with Operation Warp Speed to try to get one for the United States and nobody else, but cooperative measures of the kind that are being at least discussed in the international consortium that the United States quit.

That's the way research should be conducted. It should all be open research, not controlled by a particular corporation for themselves. Open, so everyone can use it and benefit from it. That's how research should be done all the time, crucially when it's such an urgent situation as this one. There is no reason why that can't happen.

Trump just got the best possible medical treatment, not available to anyone else, including the use of drugs for which there will be a monopoly. It doesn't have to be that way. They can be open and available to anyone, and they should be. That's the way a decent world ought to work.

We happen to have a wrecker in office who wants to destroy everything possible, everything in sight, if it's not his.

The world cares. The extent to which the world is frightened of the rogue state on the rampage is remarkable. Take the world's major business newspaper, the *Financial Times*. You can't find a more sober, respected commentator in the world than their writer Martin Wolf. He is careful, not given to exaggeration, highly regarded. He just wrote a column saying, "If the US re-elects Donald Trump, this will be terminal."[9] And he wasn't even talking about the major crises. He was talking about the crisis of international affairs, which is serious but doesn't rank anywhere near the ones we're talking about. But reelection of Trump will be terminal. That's on minor crises from one of the most sober voices in the world.

No matter the outcome of the presidential election, tens of millions are going to vote for Trump. That in and of itself is very disturbing.

It is. But ask yourself why. These are people who have basically one source of information. It comes in different packages. It comes from Fox News, Rush Limbaugh, Breitbart, talk radio. They are bombarded all the time with essentially the same message. The message is—Rush Limbaugh put it very well—there are four corners of deceit: government, academia, media, and science. They all survive on deceit. Don't pay any attention to them. Pay attention to the magician behind the curtain, our god Trump, "the chosen one," as he calls himself, the one who was sent to Earth to save Israel from Iran, according to the sycophant who is his secretary of state, Mike Pompeo.[10] They can hear the same from evangelical mega-preachers.

The result? You can see it. Almost half think that global warming isn't even taking place. Among the rest of Republicans, a small minority think it's an urgent problem. A great number think the pandemic is a liberal hoax that was sent by China to try to destroy us. If that's the kind of story you have pounded into you day and night, and you never hear anything else, and you've got this very skilled con man standing up in front of you holding up a sign saying, "I love you, I defend you," while with the other hand he stabs you in the back—if that's what you're faced with all the time, yeah, you might vote for him.

Evangelicals comprise a huge voting bloc, 25 percent of the population. He throws them crumbs. Supreme Court justices. Pastors who can preach political messages from the pulpit, a pretense—it's a total pretense, of course—to be antiabortion. Throw them all that. You can keep a constituency in line that way.

Actually, I should say this is all evoking childhood memories. Adoring crowds who worshipped Hitler at the Nuremberg rallies or Mussolini at his rallies. You hear that again when you watch a Trump rally. There is a striking difference, however. Hideous as fascist and Nazi policies were—and they were beyond description—they were at least bringing something to the people adoring the dear leader. The economies were improving. They reconstructed the economies. They were winning victories. Horrible, hideous victories, but at least victories.

What's Trump doing for his constituency? He's destroying them. He's offering them nothing. They're getting smashed worse and worse by his policies. They still adore him in the manner in which I heard at Nuremberg rallies when I was a kid. It's a very remarkable commentary on the culture and the society.

How does this connect with Richard Hofstadter in his book *Anti-Intellectualism in American Life* **and another book that he wrote, both in the 1960s,** *The Paranoid Style in American Politics,* **which looked at how fringe groups can influence politics?**[11]

I never liked those theses. For one thing, the most paranoid group in American life is elite liberal intellectuals. Take a look at the Truman Doctrine, take a look at NSC-68. Total crazed hysteria, ridiculous lies, conscious lies, in order, as Senator Arthur Vandenberg put it, to "scare the hell out of the American people."[12]

I don't have to go through that record again. It practically destroyed the world. It caused hideous atrocities in Latin America. That's the paranoid style at work. That's leading intellectuals.

Yes, you see it among the population that is mesmerized by Breitbart and Fox News. But we can't just say it's only there. It goes well beyond.

Magical thinking is probably as old as the hills, but do you think the current surge in it is connected to the growth of social media?

First of all, I should say I'm speaking as an outsider. I don't use social media. But judging from what I see, it seems to me it's a double-edged sword. Almost all the activist organizing takes place on social media. Black Lives Matter organizing, for example. Much of it seems to be on social media. On the other hand, it does provide a refuge for truly malevolent developments to take place—QAnon, Proud Boys, all of this stuff.

Even you and me, I'm sure that, to the extent that we use the internet, we tend to move toward the kinds of sources that reinforce our beliefs. That's not a good thing. You should have a wide range of exposure. But it's pretty natural—and social media magnifies this tendency—to move toward what you believe.

There's good reasons for that, and also bad effects. The bad effects are just driving people into bubbles, where you hear nothing but what you believe, reinforced. You get your news from Facebook, which is a shallow filtering of the filtering that goes on in the main media sources, which at least have some range. All of that is pretty harmful.

As I'm sure you know, there are universities now where the administration is putting plaques on the sidewalks saying, "Look Up!" In other words, don't just stare into that thing in your hand. Talk to somebody, look at your surroundings.

In terms of censorship, there are calls for social media conspiracy theory sites to be shut down. How do you stand on that kind of action?

I can see the argument for it, but I think we should be very wary of it. For one thing, I think it probably has almost no effect. There are so many ways to get around it. People will quickly find them. And it also builds up the belief that these liberal fascists are trying to wipe out us honest Americans. It feeds that story.

The other thing is just principle. I don't think the right way to deal with horrendous ideas is to try to shut them up. It's to expose them and combat them.

Let's take so-called deplatforming. Somebody is invited to a university whose views you think are horrendous. There are two ways of approaching it. One way, drive them off campus—which is a tremendous gift to them and to the right wing generally, for obvious reasons. We've seen it over and over again. There is another approach. Let them come to campus, set up meetings where you expose them, and counter their arguments. In fact, invite them to your meetings. Of course, they won't come. Raise questions to them and so on. That's educational, that's the way to counter this.

The fighting in the southern Caucasus might be an example of what Edward Said called "unresolved geographies," a legacy of imperial cartographers.[13] Stalin, as commissar of nationalities in 1920, to placate Turkey, gave Nagorno-Karabakh, which Armenians call Artsakh and Nakhchivan, both Armenian-majority areas, over to Azerbaijan. Then, with the collapse of the Soviet Union in the early 1990s, fighting breaks out, resulting in Armenian forces taking Nagorno-Karabakh. There have been skirmishes and so-called incidents on and off since then. But the attack by Azerbaijan, which began on September 27, no doubt in coordination with Turkey, represents a major escalation. The reporting here, the little that there is, is without historical background or context. Fighting erupts, they are ancient enemies, etc. What are the roots of this conflict?

Azerbaijan surely has Turkish backing, as you say. Israeli arms are pouring in. People observing Ben Gurion Airport have reported seeing Ilyushin planes coming in and out while virtually no other planes are flying, sending Israeli arms to Azerbaijan so they can kill people in Nagorno-Karabakh that are mostly Armenian. So, yes, this is an escalation.

Russia is in on both sides. Iran is supporting Armenia. It's a very dangerous situation and it's horrible for the people there. It's a time for international diplomacy and negotiations to take place to try to dampen down the tensions.

The actors involved are not the nicest people in the world, to put it mildly. Recep Tayyip Erdoğan in Turkey is basically trying to recreate something like the Ottoman caliphate, with him as the caliph, the supreme leader, throwing his weight around all over the place, destroying the remnants of democracy in Turkey at the same time.

Israel is interested only in selling arms. They will sell them to anybody, no matter who they're killing. That's the mainstay of their economy—security and arms.

And right near where I live, in Tucson, the Mexican border is being fortified with the crucial assistance of Israeli forces and corporations. Elbit Systems, in this case.

You can only hope that there will be an international effort to dampen down the atrocities and the aggression before it really explodes into massive massacres on the scene and possibly international war, because many powerful international forces are involved. It's not an easy situation to resolve, but through reasonable negotiations there could be a process that possibly could be undertaken throughout Central Asia, the Caucasus, and the Middle East.

The roots of this conflict go way back. You're right that Stalin drew the borders, but remember, he was not the only one. The entire Middle East was carved up by French and British imperialists who drew lines to their benefit, taking no account of the needs and interest of the populations. That's a large part of the cause for the bitter, violent conflicts raging through the region.

Take, say, Iraq. The British drew the borders around Iraq so that Britain, not Turkey, the former Ottoman Empire, would have control of the rich oil resources in the north. That brought together

Kurds and Arabs, who had nothing to do with each other. The British, furthermore, wanted to make sure that the new creation they were imposing would not be independent, so they carved out the principality of Kuwait, which the British would control, to prevent Iraq from having easy access to the Gulf.

Syria, Lebanon, Palestine—all have borders drawn by French and British imperialists for their interests. All over Africa you see straight lines. Why? The imperial powers were destroying Africa in their interests. Hideous atrocities. Today, people are dying in the Mediterranean fleeing from the horrors that were created. So, it's not just Stalin. All the imperial powers did this.

Turkey is also shuttling ISIS jihadi fighters from Syria and paying their salaries to go and fight with the Azerbaijanis against the Armenians.

That's apparently true. In fact, Turkey is probably doing the same in Libya, one of the other places where Erdoğan is trying to demonstrate his power.

Armenia in 2018 had a peaceful democratic revolution led by Nikol Pashinyan that overthrew the ruling oligarchy. This is one of the few instances of a nonviolent revolution replacing an autocratic regime in the post-Soviet states. It wasn't well reported on here in the United States.

As far as I know, there was essentially no interest in the United States. If there was, I failed to detect it. Yes, it was for once, apparently, a real democratic revolution.

Let's turn to the upcoming election and all the trepidation and fear surrounding it. What will happen on Election Day and the days after? Will there be a peaceful outcome? It's kind of amazing that we're even using this kind of terminology and vocabulary.

It is amazing that the question is being raised. With very rare exceptions, this hasn't happened in three hundred and fifty years of parliamentary democracy in Britain and the United States. It's astonishing that the question is raised, not by you and me, but right at the centers of the establishment. The things that are being discussed and said are almost unimaginable.

To take one striking example, two highly respected senior military commanders, now retired, Army lieutenant colonels John Nagl and Paul Yingling, recently released a public open letter to the chairman of the joint chiefs of staff, General Milley, the top military officer in the country, reviewing for him his constitutional duties in case what they call "a lawless president" decides not to leave office after an electoral defeat and mobilizes paramilitary groups to protect him from being evicted from office.[14]

They say, in that event, you took an oath of office to "support and defend the Constitution of the United States against all enemies, foreign and domestic." That's the phrase. Now, you're facing a domestic enemy that is intending to overthrow the constitutional order. It is your duty under the oath you have taken to send in military forces, they say "a brigade of the 82nd Airborne" to forcefully disperse what they say is Trump's army, his paramilitary forces, and to remove him from office. That's your duty on January twentieth if the defeated candidate, President Trump, refuses to leave office and mobilizes forces to try to protect him.

I haven't the slightest idea what the chances of this happening are. To me, it sounds unimaginable, but maybe my imagination isn't fertile enough. The crucial fact is that people are talking about it seriously in very high places. I'm sure you saw Barton Gellman's long, detailed article in the *Atlantic* about how the Republican machine is becoming organized with collections of lawyers and all sorts of others to find a way to finagle their candidate into office after he loses: discredit the election, discredit mail voting, challenge everything with all sorts of lawsuits, see if you can drag it out long enough to turn it over to the House of Representatives.[15]

The Constitution does allow under certain circumstances for the issue to go to the House. In the House, the Democrats are a large majority. The constitutional rules say each state has one vote. When you look at the distribution of states, I think it's twenty-six of them that have Republican governors. So, they could get at voting for the defeated candidate in the House.

Then you come to January 2. Two candidates appear and say, "I'm president." One of them is surrounded by a private army of para-militaries. What happens then? That's what the Republican Party is planning. Trump happens to be its leader, but it's not just him. The rot goes much deeper than Trump. He's turned, as the *New England Journal of Medicine* you quoted, "a crisis . . . into a tragedy."[16] But the crisis is there. It's a deep rot at the center of the society.

We should recognize that even apart from Trump, if this malignancy had never appeared, we would still be facing a constitutional crisis, and a very serious one. In the eighteenth century, the Constitution was a progressive document. Now it is so reactionary that if the United States tried to join the European Union with our current constitutional system, we would be rejected by the European Court of Justice. We're slaves to a document that was progressive in its time but now has features that can't be accepted in any moderately democratic society.

The worst case is the Senate. Wyoming has about half a million people, two votes. California has thirty-nine million people, two votes.

The Republican constituency—not only through control of small states but also in the demographic arrangements in the major states—happens to have predominant power to such an extreme that probably about 15 to 20 percent of the population could pretty much run the government—older, white, male, Christian, super-religious, traditional, gun-loving, evangelical. That sector is there. It's a shrinking minority, a small minority that could run things.

Remember, the Senate was established by James Madison. He understood what he was doing. Madison, like the framers generally, was very frightened of democracy. He wanted to block it. The Senate was to be the major decision-making group in the constitutional system. It was to be constituted of, as Madison put it, "the wealth of the nation," those who were sympathetic to property owners and their rights. That's who should run the country. John Jay, the first chief justice, put it, "Those who own the country ought to govern it."[17] That's the principle of the Constitution. It's been carried over.

There have been many struggles about it. The effort to crush democracy has been overcome in many ways, but much of it is still there. This is a constitutional order that's not going to survive, especially with the changes taking place.

That's assuming that we survive at all. And that's up for grabs. It's a very dramatic fact that in the Republican and Democratic conventions that just took place, we heard nothing about the major crisis of the increasing threat of nuclear war. Nothing about that. And very little about the other existential crisis we face, the race toward environmental catastrophe.

We've got to deal with that within the next ten or twenty years. If that's not handled, we're finished. The changes that are taking place in the atmosphere are permanent, and they're escalating. You can fantasize about potential geoengineering. You can imagine that for years from now, but not in the foreseeable future in a way that will have anything to do with these catastrophes.

We know how to solve them, all of them. The means are within our hands, they're feasible. But just as in the case of the pandemic, it's not enough to know. You have to do something about it.

In addition to the Electoral College, another bizarre aspect of the US system is the interregnum between the first Tuesday in November, the election, and the inauguration on January 20. That's almost three months. Anything could happen in that period.

Paul Krugman happened to have a column in the *New York Times* today warning that if Trump is not elected, and if—and it's a big if—he concedes, by no means certain, he has three months to apply his wrecking ball.[18] Out of spite, he might just devastate the economy.

Actually, there's something we must bear in mind about President Trump, which is brought up in the Nagl-Yingling letter. He may be facing serious criminal charges if he's out of office and loses immunity. He has a personal reason to hang on.

Let's return to the ecocatastrophe that is now in our face, much earlier than predicted: wildfires, hurricanes, floods, Arctic and Greenland ice melting. September was the hottest month on record. Death Valley had the highest-ever recorded temperature on Earth, 130 degrees Fahrenheit. We are hurtling toward climate catastrophe.

Every prediction of the IPCC, the Intergovernmental Panel on Climate Change, the UN agency, has turned out to be too conservative, not alarmist enough. Highly respected leading scientists are warning us we should panic now.

The deadliest effects of environmental catastrophe are in the distance. A huge rise in sea level, that's going to happen slowly, not tomorrow. But early signs of catastrophe are indeed around us, as you mentioned. It's going to get much worse. We don't know how much. There is a margin of error. But every serious analysis predicts extreme danger, maybe an end to the possibility of organized human life. Not tomorrow, maybe at the end of the century, maybe a couple of centuries.

But we have the fate of the future in our hands. We have maybe ten or twenty years to overcome it. The means to overcome it are available. Robert Pollin, an economist at the University of Massachusetts, has done very detailed, careful studies. They're being implemented in some states and countries. There is very convincing evidence that, by investing maybe 2 percent to 3 percent of gross domestic product, we could bring all of this under control. Other analysts, like Jeffrey Sachs at Columbia University, using somewhat different models, have come up with quite similar estimates. There is a very high probability that if we use the right measures, which are available and feasible, we can put a hold on the race to disaster and—and this is crucial—create a much better world, a world with better jobs, better lives, better circumstances to live in, and better institutions.

All of this is within reach. But you have to reach for it.

If we are cursed with another four years of Trump, it might be too late. We might be past or approaching irreversible tipping points. At the very best, the chances to deal with this crisis within the short time that we have will be severely lessened.

You mentioned Robert Pollin. You and he have written a new book called *Climate Crisis and the Global Green New Deal*. You cite a famous observation from Antonio Gramsci that "the old is dying and the new cannot be born; in this interregnum, a great variety of morbid symptoms appear." And then you comment, "But such morbid symptoms are countered by rising activism. . . . The new has not yet been born, but it is emerging in many intricate ways and it is far from clear what form it will take."[19]

In terms of the kind of activism that's required now and the urgency of activism and citizen engagement, how do we break the grip of what you call "capitalist logic"?

You can't break the grip of it entirely, but you can modify it. It's not a secret. What's called capitalism is actually a kind of state capitalism. No country is capitalist. A capitalist society would self-destruct so quickly it couldn't exist. Business wouldn't allow it. So, every existing society is one or another form of state capitalism. They can be more malevolent; they can be more benevolent.

Within the existing, the relevant time span, a couple of decades, we're not going to overthrow capitalist institutions, but we could seriously change them. It's perfectly possible, for example, to have a carbon tax—not of the kind that's been proposed but a really serious carbon tax in which, say, 75 percent of the revenue would go back to working people and people who need it, a redistributive carbon tax. Then you wouldn't get what you're getting in France with the Yellow Vest protests, the *Mouvement des gilets jaunes*.

Emmanuel Macron tried to institute a rise in fuel taxes and was met with a rebellion from people who rightly say it's the poor and the working people who pay this, way out of proportion, and they're the ones who need the relief, not the further burden. So not that kind of carbon tax, but the kind that is politically correct and viable because it will redistribute the revenue to the population and cut back on the profits of those who are destroying the environment.

We have to change consciousness. I just happened to look at this morning's *New York Times*. There is an article, one of a million—you see them every day—on the wondrous new developments in the eastern Mediterranean.[20] Chevron bought up a smaller company, which can now exploit what they call Israel's— it actually should be Palestine's—huge petroleum resources and pour more poison into the world. Euphoric. Look how wonderful this is. We can increase the destruction of the atmosphere. You see that daily. What does that tell people?

We can raise consciousness among liberal intellectuals enough so we don't have things like that. We can take over the fossil fuel industries. Not nationalize them. The nationalized fossil fuel industries, like Saudi Arabia and others, are worse than the private ones. But socialize them. Put them in the hands of the workforce in the community. Have them turn to things that have to be done, ranging from capping wells that the corporations have left open because they don't give a damn, but which matter for us, to shifting to working on sustainable energy, which they know how to do.

We might bear in mind that the leading force in the environmental movement forty years ago was Tony Mazzocchi's Oil, Chemical and Atomic Workers Union, the labor movement. They're the ones who are being harmed by the destructive production of polluting, destroying elements. Mazzocchi was in the lead of this, with his union behind him. That can happen again. It can happen right in the oil industry, cutting it back year by year a certain percentage until you get rid of it, say, by mid-century, turning to more economical, more beneficial, sustainable energy.

Oil and petroleum workers, there aren't very many of them, but they could be in the forefront of this.

There are many things we could be moving to. Take the automobile industry. Instead of cluttering up the highways, making traffic jams to get to work, producing more pollutants because Trump is eliminating regulations. Instead of that, auto workers could be developing efficient mass transportation. It not only saves the environment, it's a better life. Taking convenient mass transportation to work is a lot more pleasant than sitting in a traffic jam and polluting the environment. Homes can be weatherized, insulated, shifting to solar energy instead of wasting fossil fuels. It actually saves you a lot of money, gives you a pleasanter life, and saves the environment.

There are endless things that can be done across the board: individual, state, local, federal, international. There ought to be an international effort. There are no borders to global warming.

We should bear in mind that almost half the emissions in the future are going to come from what's called the developing societies, the poorer societies. They need help in transitioning to much more efficient, cheaper, more beneficial, sustainable energy. But in the initial stages, they need help. One of the parts of the Paris negotiations, which were nowhere near enough but were at least something, was to offer help to developing nations to move toward sustainable energy. The Republicans generally don't want it. Trump just killed it. Absolutely not. We're not going to help anyone save ourselves and the world.

This kind of malignancy has to be overcome. That has to be dealt with on every level, from an individual putting LED lights in their home to international efforts. What the federal government does is critically important. All of that is within our hands. It doesn't require a major social revolution. The means are all there, even without substantial institutional change.

My own view is, yes, we should overcome the profound flaws that are built into the capitalist system itself. It's not an alternative to these other steps, it's complementary. You do both at the same time. But the urgent problem of overcoming the existential crises—global warming, nuclear war, pandemics—has to be done within the general framework of existing institutions. We can improve them. But you won't be able to overcome them in the relevant time frame.

That's life. You can't get everything you want immediately. You can do the best you can—and there's a lot that we can do.

You've outlined some of those opportunities to break the grip of capitalism in your forthcoming book *Consequences of Capitalism*, written with Marv Waterstone, who is your colleague at the University of Arizona.[21]

But let me conclude with a very serious question that people have asked me, and that is about your dogs, their names, and do they share your politics, crucially?

Unfortunately, I can't say their names. Right now, they are under my desk. If I say their names, there will be a mad rush to the door. And I can't even spell their names because they've learned how to spell. So, I'll have to do it encrypted someday.

How about their politics?

I haven't really quizzed them, but they seem to be tolerating endless interviews quietly, so I guess they're not objecting too much. [*laughter*]

CLASS STRUGGLE OR GET IT IN THE NECK

Oro Valley, Arizona   November 30, 2020

The pandemic. National Public Radio is reporting "a pretty dire picture around the country," and notes, "hospital resources around the country are stretched thin."[1] The *New York Times* just headlined a story, "As Surge Spreads, No Corner of Nation Is Spared."[2] With people ignoring advice from the Centers for Disease Control and Prevention about traveling and gathering in large numbers, there'll be more grim milestones in the offing: two hundred thousand dead, four hundred thousand dead, etc. If this is not a national emergency, I don't know what is. What must be done?

What has to be done is to follow the advice of the scientists and of the countries that have successfully managed the pandemic. It is not inevitable.

We can see this from the fact that other countries, rich and poor, have handled it pretty well. China, for example, is just back to work. There are very few cases. Vietnam, right on the border of China, almost no cases. New Zealand, basically under control. Australia, pretty much under control. Taiwan, Senegal, Kenya, the Nordic countries are not too bad.

There are very diverse countries, which tells us that it is possible, but not without leadership that most of the time even denies

107

that it's happening. That filters down to the population. We've seen reports of people dying of COVID-19 in hospital beds in the Dakotas and telling the nurses that it's all a hoax, it's not happening.[3] You drive around—I mostly stay home, but I drive sometimes—and you see people congregating in supermarket malls with no masks.

What about the notion you hear in some circles of individual freedom versus collective responsibility?

Individual freedom is a curious idea. Do you have the freedom to drive on the left side of the road if you feel like it? Do you have the freedom to run around malls shooting an assault rifle? That's what it means to go to a public area without wearing a mask. That's threatening people's lives, seriously. That's not individual freedom. That's unacceptable license.

Nobody accepts the kinds of things I described. If you want a choice not to wear a mask, that's okay—stay home, don't endanger others.

At some point, soon hopefully, there will be vaccines. But how do we want to come out of this pandemic and attendant economic crisis?

There will be vaccines. There are some that are already in pretty advanced stages of testing. The most advanced, as far as I know, is almost unmentionable in the United States, the Chinese vaccine. They're already using it on large numbers of people, though that may or may not be good practice. I'm not in a position to judge, but it's apparently pretty advanced, and it's taken seriously by US scientists. We don't hear about it. It won't be available here if it works.

There are vaccines being developed here, what's called the "Pfizer vaccine," which actually was developed by two Turkish immigrants in Germany and then marketed by Pfizer. There's the Moderna vaccine. There's an Oxford vaccine. Others may come along. Then comes the questions: Will people take them? Can they be distributed to the people who need them?

There are policy choices that relate to this. So, for example, there is an international consortium, COVAX (COVID-19 Vaccines Global Access), 170 or so countries that have been working on trying to develop cooperation in vaccine development, which is obviously the best way. Data should be shared freely, not sequestered by particular private corporations and governments that support them. There should be no monopolization of vaccines. There should be distribution arranged to the people around the world who need them, not those rich enough to buy them. All of these things, at least in principle, are the working agenda of COVAX.

How well it's being honored we could ask, but at least that's the agenda. But the United States has pulled out.[4] The United States is not alone. Some of the European countries are trying to monopolize any vaccine that comes along, too.

Then comes the question of taking the vaccine. A large number of people in the United States say, "We're just not going to accept this. We don't want the government to intrude on our personal lives. I don't believe the science." There's a big anti-vaccine movement in the United States, which has a lethal effect in a rich country like this. If this sentiment spreads in poorer countries, it'll just be lethal.

The anti-vaccine movement is rooted in understandable contempt for—or at least distrust in—government, but it shouldn't reach to this domain. And that's going to be a serious problem, even if the vaccine is developed and is available. The United States is unusual, almost unique in not having a general health system. So, it's not clear that if a vaccine is available, it'll be affordable or that there'll be places where people can go to get it. That takes national coordination.

The Trump administration has, of course, refused to coordinate this. It remains to be seen whether a Biden administration will carry out a plan. Until just a few days ago, Trump had refused even to share data with the incoming Biden administration.[5] That, of course, makes any reaction slower and more ineffective.

There should be major pressures to accelerate, firstly, the development of procedures to restrict and mitigate the spread of the virus, and secondly, to make sure that when vaccines are available, they'll be essentially free, that there will be distribution to those who need them, who will be encouraged to take them, rather than being told that the vaccine is a hoax and that the disease is a hoax.

We're living in a country where a large part of the population is just in extreme denialism. If you can believe the polls, over three quarters of Republicans think the election was stolen.[6] Huge percentages think global warming is not a serious problem. That is an extraordinary problem. The denial of the pandemic is also significant.

In such an atmosphere, it's going to be very hard to deal with extremely serious problems.

Let's talk about the November 3 election, the record turnout of 150 million people, the success of voting by mail and early voting. A bit of euphoria, if I could use that term, as the autocrat is replaced. Now we can go back to things as they were, a kind of restoration. A sigh of relief was audible in establishment circles and from media pundits like David Brooks, Thomas Friedman, and Mark Shields. You wrote to me a few days after the election. You said of the results, "Relief, but no celebration. Depressing to see Democrats blow it again." What did you mean by that? The Democrats had plenty of money. What happened to the Blue Wave?

The Democrats lost to an incredible degree. They lost at every level, except for the presidency. And the presidency was a vote against Trump, even by many of the wealthy, the corporate sector, who were tired of his antics. But at every other level, Congress, state legislatures, local elections, they lost and lost badly.

If you think of the circumstances, it's astonishing that Trump was even able to run. Here's somebody who had just killed tens, if not hundreds of thousands of Americans through malevolent practice, let alone all of his other crimes. And he's running for president, considered a viable candidate. And not only that, but the whole ticket that supported him won at every level.

It's an amazing defeat for the Democrats. Not that the Democrats are all that great, but just in terms of party politics, it was a shocking failure. I think you can see why. The Democrats devoted their campaign efforts to try to swing some affluent suburbs toward them. Well, maybe they succeeded in that. But that's not enough to develop any sort of electoral strategy. In fact, this has been going on since Obama. Since Obama, the Democratic Party has pretty much abandoned its activities at the local and state levels, just doesn't bother. It's a party of Wall Street, rich professionals, and so on. The others will take care of themselves.

And you could see this in particular cases. There's been a lot of discussion about the quite remarkable Democratic Party losses in South Texas on the border, largely a Mexican American community. These are areas that hadn't voted for a Republican for a century, literally, since Warren Harding, and Trump did quite well, even won in some areas—a dramatic reversal.

A number of analyses have been put forth. If you read liberal commentators, they say that Biden lost it because of the terrible gaffe in the final presidential debate. You'll recall, at the end of the last debate, Biden said something that had liberal commentators just shocked. What was the mistake? He said, we have to do something to prevent the human species from being destroyed. That's basically what he said. Those weren't his words. His words were, "I would transition from the oil industry," which is equivalent to saying, "we have to do something to try to make it likely at least that human society can survive."[7] That was a horrible gaffe, and it affected the oil-producing economies like the ones in South Texas because people feel—you hear it from interviews and so on—that the Democrats are going to take my life away, take away my job, my community, my businesses, and so on, just because some pointy-headed liberals claim that there's a climate crisis.

Now, of course, the gaffe was not saying it loudly and clearly. We have to say that loud and clear. We have to transition from a fossil fuel economy within a couple of decades, which means not delaying, starting now, cutting back each year so that, say, by mid-century, we've finished with fossil fuels. That has to be said strongly and persuasively.

So, what do you do about the oil producing sectors? What do you do about South Texas or areas where there's fracking in Pennsylvania? You don't just say, "Sorry, folks, you've got to lose your jobs and your business and everything else because we say there's a climate crisis." What you do is go down there and organize. You explain to people what it means. It means, first of all, that this is inevitable, and we have to do it. Your children and grandchildren will be consigned to hell if we don't.

Secondly, there's an effective way to make this transition that will improve your lives, give you better jobs, more jobs, a more livable environment, better community, and better health. Here are the ways. Spell them out.

It happens to be true, and it can be done. But not if the Democratic National Committee is devoting its efforts to convincing a couple of affluent suburban women to shift their vote.

You have to be down in South Texas organizing. And in the places where there was mostly Latino organizing, it was effective. Near where I live, in Maricopa County, Arizona, there has been extensive organizing with Latino leadership for several years, and they voted against Trump.

The same is true of many other issues. Take the Democrats who are claiming that the election was lost because the crazy leftists were saying, "defund the police." When I think about that for a minute, if you just say, "defund the police," you're going to lose. You're telling people, "I want you to have no protection if somebody breaks into your home." Nobody wants to hear that. On the other hand, if you give the actual substantive meaning of "defund the police," as Bernie Sanders and a couple of others tried to do, it's a sensible, attractive program, which people will support and which the police will support. Take away from the police responsibilities that they should never have in the first place—in fact, the large majority of their responsibilities. Police shouldn't be involved in domestic disputes, mental health problems, lost dogs, or drug overdoses, and so on. That's not police business. These things all should be handled by community services under community control, which can do them better.

So, defund the police by taking away those responsibilities. Next step, as Sanders himself tried to emphasize, increase salaries for police, make it a better occupation, make better conditions for policing, so the police can do the things that, in fact, any community is going to need, but not other things and not running around with heavy weapons terrorizing people. That's "defund the police."

But if you just scream the slogan, nobody hears that. What they hear is, "You don't care if people break into my home." People, by implication, Black people, that's the message.

If you want to be serious about achieving goals, you have to pay attention to your tactics. That's crucial. Tactics aren't just something insignificant at the fringe. Any activist and organizer should know this. It should be their second nature that this is what matters. How do you approach people? How do you get them to understand what you're trying to say, what you think is for their benefit and the benefit of others? Not by shouting a slogan. It takes work. It takes direct organizing and activism.

It's interesting the alacrity with which establishment Democrats blame their poor showing on, as you mentioned, not by name, Alexandria Ocasio-Cortez, Rashida Tlaib, Ilhan Omar, Ayanna Pressley, and some other young representatives, many of them women.

Anthony DiMaggio, who has done some of the best work on these topics for years, had a recent study of the latest available data on voting patterns that confirms what's been reported elsewhere.[8] Trump won remarkably high votes in almost any demographic you consider—not out of range for what it's been in the past, but remarkably high—in one, particularly, as DiMaggio has shown before. The main support for Trump is the relatively affluent—not super rich, but relatively affluent, way above the median, in the $100,000 to $200,000 income range. That's not working people, contrary to illusions. The median income in the United States is around $70,000. That's median. Lower than that, Trump does poorly.

And when you go to higher incomes, it's sort of split. Rich professionals are split. The very wealthy in this election are somewhat split because of concern about the way Trump's harming their interests in the economy.

The range of $100,000 to $200,000 was the base for Trump's support, but seems to be increased substantially since 2016. I should say that's kind of a mystery. I don't understand whether it should be true, but it happened, and we should think about it. There's a lot of problems for the left to deal with if it hopes to make any progress.

One, of course, is that the incoming Biden administration is very much a mixed story. Among the economic advisers and appointees, it's not too bad. People like Heather Boushey, Jared Bernstein, Janet Yellen could be very positive appointments. Others much less so. And across the board, there's lots to object to. Just getting rid of Trump is a major victory, but it's not going to mean very much if you can't implement policies that are substantive and effective in dealing with the massive crisis that exists.

Talk about the Supreme Court and the power of Mitch McConnell, who rammed through the Amy Coney Barrett nomination, giving the court a decisive right-wing majority, perhaps

for decades. What do you think about proposals for term limits for Supreme Court justices or expanding the number of justices? Or statehood for Puerto Rico and the District of Columbia, which would increase the number of senators by four. Or do you think these are just time-consuming dead ends, given the structure of politics?

Those are all important reforms. But, remember, the Supreme Court is only part of the judiciary problem. For ten years now, McConnell has been working hard to ensure that the entire judiciary, top to bottom, will be staffed by young, ultra-right Federalist Society–approved lawyers who will be able to maintain the ultra-reactionary McConnell-Trump-style programs for a generation by simply blocking everything else at every level. That's been a main function of the Senate—first, blocking Obama's nominees, and second, ramming through the huge number of ultra-right young nominees during the Trump years. And it's been very effective. You look at the numbers, it's astonishing. McConnell has essentially eliminated the Senate as a deliberative body, theoretically once famously described as the world's greatest deliberative body. Okay, you can argue about that. But at least the term meant something.

Now, the House sends measures to the Senate, and they don't even look at them. What they do is two things. One task is to pass legislation to benefit the corporate sector and the very rich, from deregulation to the incredible tax scam. The other is to staff the judiciary with the far right. So, it's not just the Supreme Court.

I think admitting Puerto Rico and the District of Columbia should be done, for lots of reasons. But it's going to be very hard to achieve that with a Republican Senate or to achieve anything with McConnell as leader of the Senate. The idea that you can somehow make friends with them and cooperate, that's a joke. They're out for blood. They don't want to cooperate. They want to make the country ungovernable, so that they can come back into power at every level below the president. I think that's what we're going to be seeing for the next couple of years—basically an extension of what's going on now.

Howard Zinn said, "It would be naive to depend on the Supreme Court to defend the rights of poor people, women, people of color, dissenters of all kinds. Those rights only come alive when citizens organize, protest, demonstrate, strike, boycott, rebel, and violate the law in order to uphold justice."[9]

That's pretty much what the historical record shows. You can go back to the Constitution. By the standards of the eighteenth century, the Constitution was moderately progressive, but it was not what the population wanted. It is well described in the major scholarly study of the formation of the Constitution, Michael Klarman's book *The Framers' Coup*, the coup of the framers against democracy.[10] That's an excellent book, incidentally—the scholarly gold standard—very good reading. You can see in it, step by step, how James Madison, Alexander Hamilton, and other major figures in framing the Constitution were primarily concerned about the popular democratic thrust among the general population.

A lot of it played out on issues that most people don't pay much attention to. There was a huge struggle, for example, about paper money during the American Revolution. The government had huge debts. How were they going to be paid off? Well, one proposal was to put it on the shoulders of the population. Make them pay for it, not the rich speculators. We want to preserve their rights. That's the way the Constitution was framed. The population wanted paper money, so the currency could be inflated to help pay off the debts. Speculators would suffer from it, but the population would gain. That was one major part of the formation of the Constitution.

Another part was Madison's realization that the Senate should represent, in his words, "the wealth of the nation," the most responsible group of men, those who have sympathy with property owners and their rights. So, the Senate was given predominant power among the various components of the government.

It was not elected. It was picked by electors from the legislature, which could be trusted to make sure that the wealthy would be in charge. And many other measures were proposed with the main purpose of preventing democracy, including the creation of large legislative districts where people wouldn't be able to get together. Remember, this is the days of the horse and carriage when it was hard to get around.

Lots of detailed measures were taken to reduce the threat of democracy and to carry out the framers' coup against democracy. But there was a problem. The population didn't accept it. You had lots of ferment, the kinds of things that Howard Zinn was talking about: uprisings and efforts to win more democratic rights of all sorts and forms.

This struggle continues throughout US history. The Supreme Court, which you mentioned, is a good example. The Supreme Court has overwhelmingly been on the side of wealth and power. Not totally—there were breaks. But that's been the strong tendency. It's a conservative institution.

Actually, the Constitution does not say anything about the Supreme Court having the right of judicial review, having the authority to cancel legislation. That was just introduced by the court itself under Chief Justice John Marshall years later, in 1803. It's become the convention since. But these are all constant struggles.

And it's not just the courts and the government. It's also private power, which is enormous and has an immense influence on the government. Most of the population has no influence whatsoever on governmental decisions. Maybe the top 10 percent, and of them, a very small fraction, in fact. Well, that's quite apart from the formal constitutional structure. And, of course, during the neoliberal period, all of this has been strongly enhanced.

So, there's been this massive robbery of the population for forty years. That has effects on the way the government works. That's why you end up with, say, 90 percent of the population being basically unrepresented.

These struggles go on constantly. They're going to go on in the post-pandemic world. It's a radical class struggle, but one element in the struggle is always fighting: the business world. They're dedicated. They never stop. They didn't stop during the New Deal, and continued, continued afterward.

Unless working people, the general population, take part in the class struggle, they're going to get it in the neck.

This year began with the US assassination of Iranian general Qassem Suleimani, and it almost is ending with the assassination of the Iranian scientist Mohsen Fakhrizadeh, probably by Israel.[11] David Sanger, writing in the *New York Times*, reported, "The assassination ... threatens to cripple President-elect Joseph R. Biden Jr.'s effort to revive the Iran nuclear deal before he can even begin his diplomacy with Tehran." And he continues, "And that may well have been a main goal of the operation."[12] About Israeli prime minister Benjamin Netanyahu, Sanger writes that he has a second agenda: "There must be no return to the previous nuclear agreement." Nowhere in the article does Sanger even mention that Israel has nuclear weapons or that this assassination is another example of its violations of international law. What's going on with US-Iran relations in this interim period? Do you see the danger of a possible wider war?

I think that analysis is pretty plausible. It looks as if, for some time now, the Trump/Pompeo administration has been trying hard to provoke the Iranian government to carry out some kind of act that could be used as a pretext for a sharp escalation of the war against Iran.

Notice we are at war against Iran. We have a blockade. US sanctions are a serious business, US sanctions are third-party sanctions, which means everyone in the world must observe them or else.

Europe doesn't like the sanctions against Iran, but they have to observe them, or else we'll toss them out of the international financial system. We just saw this shown dramatically at the United

Nations recently. The United States went to the Security Council and requested, meaning demanded, that the Security Council renew the lapsed sanctions against Iran. Every US ally refused. Almost total refusal.[13] The US reacted. Pompeo returned to the Security Council and said, "You are reinstituting the sanctions." They obeyed.[14] You can't step on the toes of the godfather.

This is just one of the many examples where the Trump administration is trying almost desperately to get Iran to carry out some action, which they can use as a pretext probably for missile attacks against the nuclear facilities or something like that, to which Iran might respond. For example, Iran does have the missile capacity to attack the Saudi energy facilities in northeast Saudi Arabia, near the Iran border. That's the main center of global fossil fuel production. Also, Saudi Arabia's desalination facilities and others, although it would set off a huge war.

We don't know what all of this would lead to. But Washington is eager to do this to try to ensure exactly, as Netanyahu said, that we do not go back to the earlier situation.

I agree with Netanyahu, actually. We should not go back to the earlier agreement. What we should do is impose a new nuclear weapons–free zone, which really means nuclear weapons would be subject to international controls and inspection, and US aid to Israel would be questioned.

That's what we should do, not just go back to the Joint Comprehensive Plan of Action. So, in some ways, I agree with him. But we shouldn't be trapped in this narrow conception that's provided by the media and general intellectual framework. In fact, the Biden administration is playing along. One of their top appointees, National Security Advisor Jake Sullivan, recently said that the Biden administration will be willing to consider going back to the joint agreement, but the ball is in Iran's court.[15] They have to start by cutting back, by reversing their increased enrichment of uranium. And they've got to have a positive attitude toward negotiations. If they do that, we'll consider it.

Absolutely backward. We are the ones who should be pleading with Iran to go back to the negotiations, which we have consistently undermined, actually destroyed under Trump, but undermined under Obama. Even under Obama, we were not living up to the agreements. One part of the agreement is that no party shall try to injure the Iranian economy during the period of the negotiations. The Obama administration was doing it constantly. We weren't living up to the commitments. But now the Biden administration spokesman is saying, we might be willing to consider going back to the negotiations if they take the first steps, as if they're the guilty party, not us.

The journalist Robert Fisk passed away in late October. We both knew him and participated in public events with him. In 2010, he said this about objectivity: "It is the duty of a foreign correspondent to be neutral and unbiased on the side of those who suffer, whoever they may be."[16] Fisk was a critic of US foreign policy in the Middle East, the Israeli treatment of Palestinians. He wrote of the Kurdish question, the Armenian genocide, and other taboo topics. Talk about him briefly, and then this notion, this almost sacred notion of objectivity.

Fisk was a marvelous correspondent—a brave, honest, knowledgeable, great writer. Much of the profession just hated him. And now he's under very ugly attacks from many journalists. A number of good journalists have written about this, like Jonathan Cook.[17] Now that he's dead and can't sue anybody, all kinds of ugly attacks are coming from journalists. It's sick.

So, what about objectivity? It's a funny notion. First of all, we shouldn't pretend that we're just neutral observers. Every human being has a point of view. If you don't have a point of view on things, you're not a human being. You don't have a functioning brain. If you're a serious journalist or scholar, what you do is make your point of view very clear, so that your readers can understand it and compensate for it, and then try to be as accurate as you can about what's happening.

If what's important to you is the rights of the powerful, okay, make that clear and write from that perspective. If your point of view is the rights of the suffering and the oppressed, make that clear, and then describe that as accurately as you can, without cutting corners.

Pure objectivity is just a meaningless notion in the sciences, as well. No nuclear physicist approaches the next article he reads with pure objectivity, as if he didn't have some beliefs about the subject. I mean, it's just ludicrous.

I recently read a debate among a bunch of top scientists about what a particle is, the most critical concept in physics.[18] You have lots of different views, with people arguing about it. Any way they look at an experiment is going to be shaped by their point of view. That's fundamental physics.

Suppose you're looking at the Syrian war. Of course, you're going to have a point of view. But that doesn't mean you can't be a fine objective journalist, as Robert Fisk was, or like Patrick Cockburn, Charles Glass, Jonathan Steele, and quite a few others. They all have a point of view.

Fisk was also a great human being. I knew him personally for many years.

November 29 is the International Day of Solidarity with the Palestinian People, a UN-organized observance. It marks UN Resolution 181 of November 29, 1947, which proposed the partition of Palestine into two states, one Arab and one Jewish. The national poet of Palestine is Mahmoud Darwish (1941–2008). One of his greatest poems is "Under Siege." This is the opening verse:

> Here on the slopes of hills, facing the dusk and the
> cannon of time
> Close to the gardens of broken shadows,
> We do what prisoners do,

And what the jobless do:
We cultivate hope.[19]

What hope is there for the Palestinians, a people that you have been in solidarity with for decades, at what seems to be the bleakest moment in their history, when more and more land and water is being annexed by Israel and the possibility of a viable, independent Palestinian state recedes?

It is a grim moment in the history of the Palestinians. And anyone concerned with their rights and prospects has to be extremely careful about two things. One, being clear about what the actual situation is. Two, being clear about the kinds of action can be taken to try to improve, overcome, at least mitigate the crisis in which they live.

Those two things require serious clear thought, and I don't think it's being done. So, on the issue of what the circumstances are, almost all discussion these days that you see is about two options. One is a two-state settlement of some sort. There has been a general international consensus on that since the 1970s, so something like that. The other option that's considered is one state. Israel takes over the West Bank, and then an anti-apartheid struggle ensues. That's the second option.

But that's missing the third and crucial option, the one that is in fact being implemented before our eyes, which has been the major guideline for Israeli policies for fifty years. That's a "Greater Israel," in which Israel takes over whatever is of value to it in the West Bank—formerly it was Gaza, but now it's the West Bank—but evades Palestinian population concentrations. Israel does not want Nablus, doesn't want Tulkarm. Israel doesn't want Palestinians.

This is nothing like the anti-apartheid struggle. In South Africa, the white population needed the Black population, and in fact tried to subsidize the Bantustans, tried to make them look decent to the international community. This is quite different.

Israel just wants the Palestinians out. It does use them for cheap labor, but they can get cheap exploited labor from Thailand or other places—and do, in fact.

They just want the Palestinians out. What they've been doing for fifty years—and what you see before your eyes if you drive around the West Bank—is to build a greater Israel, in which Israel takes over all the valuable areas, the Jordan Valley, about a third of the territory, fertile land, and kick out the population on one or another pretext.

Take greater Jerusalem, a huge area about five times the size of what Jerusalem ever was, or take the city of Ma'ale Adumim, east of Jerusalem, built up mostly in the Clinton years. The corridor to it pretty much bisects the West Bank. Same to the north with the town of Ariel and the town of Kedumim. Leave out the Palestinian population concentrations until we finally manage to get rid of them.

The rest of the Palestinians who live in the areas that Israel is taking over, are in isolated enclaves, separated from their olive groves, agricultural areas, and herds, with checkpoints that occasionally are open at the will of Israeli soldiers. Keep them in isolation, subjected to constant attacks by what are called hilltop youth and other terrorist crazies, and just make life impossible for them.

Meanwhile, the Jewish-held areas are basically suburbs of Tel Aviv and Jerusalem. So, you can live in Ma'ale Adumim in a nice villa, subsidized by the government, and take the Jewish-only superhighway to your job in Tel Aviv, and then come back to your nice, subsidized home in the suburbs in the evening. You don't even see an Arab.

That's greater Israel. That's what's being implemented.

As in any other neocolony, the Israeli authorities understand that you have to do something for the Palestinian elites. They need a place where they can gather, go to the theater, have nice restaurants, shopping malls, and pretend they're in Europe. That's

Ramallah, basically. You find the same thing all through Africa and other similar neocolonial areas.

That's the reality. Israel is not going to accept taking over the Palestinian population. Israel is not going to accept becoming a minority state with a minority of Jews. We can be quite certain of that. So that's just not an option. There's a lot of talk about it, but I don't think it's an option. It's fine to discuss it, but it seems to me that's what has to be faced.

As far as actions are concerned that could overcome this crisis, there's one point that's critical, that's the United States. If the United States continues to support the Israeli greater Israel project, as it has pretty consistently, with some breaks, they'll just continue. There's no reason for the Israelis to stop, as long as the global godfather says, "Go ahead."

Will it continue? I think that's an open question. If you look at support for Israel within the United States, it's shifted radically over the last couple of decades. Go back twenty years, or before. Israel was the darling of the liberal population. They loved Israel. It's the most wonderful place in the world. I think this was true pretty much worldwide. Swedish teenagers could live in a kibbutz because it was so wonderful.

That's all changed. Israel is now a pariah state among liberal opinion. In fact, most people who identify as liberal Democrats are more supportive of Palestinian rights. This is also true among the younger Jewish population, I should say.

Support for Israel has shifted to the far right, as Israel itself has shifted to the far right. So, the support for Israel in the United States is now the Republican Party. It's evangelicals, ultranationalists, those connected to military industry, which has very tight links to Israel. That's the support for Israel.

And there are open possibilities for trying to shift US policy around very concrete things. We've already mentioned the legitimacy of US military and economic aid to Israel. It's a sore point. That's why nobody wants to talk about it. But it's grounds for activism. As is Israel's constant violations of international law and its huge human rights violations, including the vicious repression in the occupied territories.

All of this should be front and center. And I think with that, there could be a change in US policy. It doesn't have to be a huge change. Even bringing up the possibility of terminating or limiting the huge economic and military aid to Israel would have a big effect.

So, I think there are things that can be done. I don't think the situation is hopeless.

But you have to be clear. Ask yourself what can be done effectively, not what makes you feel righteous. It's kind of like talking about defund the police. You have to do it in a way that is going to work, not in a way that is self-destructive.

During the summer, you used to find time to read fiction.

This is in fact the first summer where I haven't had the luxury of enjoying a series of novels and other forms of relaxation. I'm just too busy. The last summer I was on a José Saramago kick, running through his novels.

Years ago, you told me you had "bad genes" and that you did not expect to live a long life. Well, you turn ninety-two on December 7. You have a Bicycle Theory of Longevity.

It's pretty simple. If you keep riding fast, you don't fall off. Unfortunately, my wife, Valéria, won't let me get near a bicycle.

CONSEQUENCES OF CAPITALISM

Oro Valley, Arizona   March 15, 2021

Consequences of Capitalism: Manufacturing Discontent and Resistance **is your new book coauthored with Marv Waterstone, your colleague at the University of Arizona. The book is based on the "What Is Politics?" course you co-taught. Talk about the book.**

Well, as you said, the book is basically an expanded record of the courses that we've taught for the past five years, both for students and for the community, on the general nature of what is politics. We look at domestic and foreign policy, world affairs, a fair amount of history, economics.

The lectures are broken up into a series. We begin with questions: what is the basis on which you come to know and believe something? How does Gramscian hegemonic common sense get imposed? How is consent manufactured, to borrow Walter Lippmann's phrase? What are the mechanisms?

Then we move on to particular areas, beginning with the ones of prime importance for survival—militarism and nuclear war, environmental destruction—and turning to a variety of domestic issues. We also focus on what social movements can achieve and how efforts are made to resist and control them.

Each week, we bring in speakers from activist movements who describe what they do, what kind of problems they face, what kinds of opportunities there are.

We keep bringing these lectures up-to-date each year. It's been a very lively experience.

You write in the preface, "Will the species survive? Will organized human life survive? Those questions cannot be avoided. There is no way to sit on the sidelines."[1]

Like it or not, that's a fact. It's this generation that will decide whether human society continues in any organized form—or whether we reach tipping points that are irreversible, and we spin off into total catastrophe. It's the same with the growing threat of nuclear weapons. There's just no alternative to deciding right now.

There are other problems. The current pandemic will somehow be controlled at enormous and needless cost of lives, but there are others coming. And they could be more serious unless we take significant steps to prepare for them.

We face other major issues of species survival—not just the human species. We are racing forward to destroy other species on an incredible scale that hasn't been seen for sixty-five million years.

We're talking on the Ides of March. You remember what the soothsayer said in Shakespeare's play *Julius Caesar*. One of the topics you discuss in the book is the connection between David Hume, an eighteenth-century Enlightenment philosopher, and Antonio Gramsci, the noted twentieth-century Marxist. What's that connection?

David Hume was a great philosopher. He wrote *Of the First Principles of Government*, one of the classic texts of what we now call political philosophy or political science. He opens his study by raising a question. He says he's surprised to see the "easiness" with which people subordinate themselves to power systems.[2] And he says that's a mystery. A mystery because the people themselves really have the power. So why do they subject themselves to masters? And he says the answer to this mystery must be consent. That the masters succeed in what we now call manufacturing consent and keep the public in line by their belief that they must subordinate themselves to power systems. And he says this miracle occurs in all societies, no matter how brutal or how free.

Hume was writing in the wake of the first democratic revolution, the English revolution of the mid-seventeenth century, which led to what we call the British constitution, a couple of words basically that says that the king will be subordinate to parliament. At the time, parliament meant merchants and manufacturers.

David Hume's close friend Adam Smith wrote about the consequences of the revolution at about the same time. In his famous book, *The Wealth of Nations*, he pointed out that the "merchants and manufacturers" of England, who now had sovereignty, are, in fact, in Smith's words, "the masters of mankind."[3] They used their power to control the government and to ensure that their own interests are very well taken care of, no matter how "grievous" the effect on the people of England, and even worse, on those who are subject to what he called the "savage injustice of the Europeans," referring mainly to the British rule in India.[4]

The same year that Smith wrote *The Wealth of Nations*, the American Revolution broke out. A couple of years later, the Constitution was formed.

The English revolution of the mid-seventeenth century is presented, as I said, as a conflict between the king and parliament. And it ended with the king being subordinate to parliament, the rising merchant and manufacturing class. But that's not the whole story.

There was also the general public, which didn't want to be ruled by either king or parliament. It was a lively period. Itinerant workers and ministers were writing pamphlets that reached much of the general public. Their pamphlets and talks called for being ruled by countrymen like ourselves, who know the people's wants, not by knights and gentlemen who only want to oppress us. They called for universal health, universal education.

They were finally crushed. So, Hume and Smith are both writing after the victory of the merchants and manufacturers, not only over the king but the general public.

This was reenacted a few years later in the US Constitution. The public wanted democracy. The Framers, wealthy men, mostly slave owners, were meeting in Philadelphia. They wanted to prevent the threat of democracy, much like "the men of best quality," as they called themselves during the first democratic revolution.

In fact, it didn't take more than a few years for Madison to realize what Adam Smith had realized before. In 1792, Madison wrote a letter to his friend Jefferson in which he deplored the collapse of the democratic system that he hoped he had established, with not too much democracy but at least some. What Madison said was that by now, the "stockjobbers"—in our day that means the financial institutions—had taken so much power that they are, as he called it, the "tool" and "tyrant" of government.[5] They both work for government and control government, and they work for their own interests, no matter how much they oppress the public. This is the seventeenth and eighteenth centuries.

Many of the same problems exist today. Gramsci gives an account of the same principles in modern terms.

Talk about the role of intellectuals, organic and traditional. The latter, sometimes called disparagingly, stenographers to power. It was Reinhold Niebuhr, the liberal theologian, who coined the phrase "responsible intellectuals." Gramsci called them "experts in legitimation."[6] And then there's of course what Henry Kissinger added to the widening definition.

The terms *responsible intellectuals* and *responsible people* come from the main liberal theorists of modern democracy. People like Walter Lippmann; Harold Lasswell, one of the founders of modern political science; Reinhold Niebuhr, considered the theologian of the liberal establishment, highly revered; Edward Bernays, one of the founders of the public relations industry.

They're called progressive theorists. They all wrote texts about how democracy should function. And the idea was similar. Actually, it's similar to what Hume and Gramsci talked about. They said that what they called the responsible men, which means responsible educated intellectuals, have to essentially maintain power. The general public, in their view, is stupid and ignorant, and cannot be left to run their own affairs. They're not capable of it. They have to be controlled by what Niebuhr called "necessary illusions" and "emotionally potent oversimplifications," so that they keep in their place.[7]

They have a place, as Lippmann put it. They are "spectators," not "participants," but they do have a role. They're supposed to show up every four years and push a lever to pick one or another of the responsible men to lead them, and then they go back to their own affairs and not bother us. We, the responsible men, are to be "free of the trampling and roar of the bewildered herd."[8] We should not, as Lasswell put it, be overcome by "democratic dogmatism" about people being able to take control, to work for their own interests. They were much too stupid and ignorant for that. We must run it.

The term *intellectual* in its modern sense was really developed during the late nineteenth century when Émile Zola and other French writers and lawyers were criticizing the gross mistreatment of Alfred Dreyfus. They were criticizing the army and the state for his sentencing on fabricated charges. They were bitterly condemned by the immortals of the French Academy for daring to criticize our great institutions and claim there was a serious miscarriage of justice.

Zola had to flee France to escape the attacks. Others were jailed. This is history. If you dare to go beyond obeisance to the powerful, you are likely to suffer in one way or another, depending on the nature of the society.

Henry Kissinger, who's a master in the art, put it pretty well himself. He said the role of the policy intellectual is to articulate the thinking of those in power. If they don't put it exactly right, we'll articulate it correctly for them.

That's the role of the serious intellectual—and that's how you become a respected, responsible intellectual.

During the Civil War, something occurs involving Ralph Waldo Emerson and Nathaniel Hawthorne. Talk about that and how it intersects with the role of intellectuals.

That was quite interesting. When the Civil War broke out, Emerson, who was the leading philosopher of the time, was very enthusiastic about the war, because he thought it would break down social structures and lead to a freer society. Not that he was in favor of the North. He was against all calls for patriotism. He criticized and denounced them. But he did hope that it would undermine repressive social structures. Very soon, he became a great enthusiast for the war. He wrote famous poems about how young people from Harvard were going out to die in order to fulfill their duty and in service to the Union.[9]

Most of the intellectuals in Concord, Massachusetts, the main intellectual center at the time, went along with Emerson. They were strongly in favor of the war. Hawthorne was one of the very few who didn't. He kept mostly quiet. But he did do something quite interesting. He went on a tour through the South in the latter days of the war. It was clear the Union was going to defeat the South. He visited Washington. He wrote about Abraham Lincoln.[10] He didn't deify him in the manner that was considered appropriate at the time. He wrote a mildly critical, mildly favorable comment. He went to prison camps, where Southern soldiers were being held. He talked to them. He wrote a major article for the *Atlantic Monthly*, the main intellectual journal of that period.[11]

In the article, I'm paraphrasing, he said, Look, these young men in those Southern prison camps, they're just ordinary people who were called to battle in a cause they thought was just. We have to treat them with dignity, as honorable human beings. And in general, he gave a very measured picture of the victory. He wasn't calling for enthusiastic triumphalist acclaim for our magnificent victory and our magnificent leaders. He was critical and serious, very muted.

Well, the *Atlantic* agreed to publish the article. But if you read it, the article is interpolated with comments from the editors denouncing Hawthorne for what he says. He wasn't laudatory enough of Lincoln. He was too favorable to these Southern soldiers in prison camps.

It's a humane and decent article. He was very sharply attacked for it. He actually died shortly after. We don't know what the repercussions were. But the distinction between him and Emerson was very sharp.

Mars is in the news. Perseverance rover is on the Red Planet, sending back photos. Years ago, you talked about a journalist from Mars. How would she cover the pandemic and the introduction of vaccines?

It's a very strange thing that's happening with the introduction of vaccines. In the United States, a substantial number of people are refusing to take it. They're overwhelmingly Republicans, and for many reasons: distrust of government, distrust of science, other objections.

But it's not restricted to the United States. So, in France, for example, according to their most recent reports, about 40 percent of people are refusing to take the vaccine. This is a strange phenomenon. There's overwhelming evidence of the importance of taking the vaccine if we want to get this plague under control. But fear and dislike of government, science, and authority has reached such points that people are taking very dangerous actions to avoid what needs to be done.

You can compare this with other countries. It varies. Australia got the disease very quickly under control. One main reason is they have a highly effective health system, which people trust. We have a dysfunctional health system. Others do, too. Secondly, they just are willing to take collective responsibility for one another. So, they accepted harsh lockdowns, which were very successful, and the disease was essentially controlled. The same has happened in New Zealand, Taiwan, and other countries.

But there are places—the United States is one, interestingly, France is another—where the discontent and distrust is so high that a great many people are just unwilling to join in the collective effort to control and put down the disease. And there are many lives being lost.

There was recently a study in the United States, which compared the city of Seattle with the general situation in the United States. Seattle is one place where the virus was pretty much well controlled by the kind of means that were successful in Australia, Taiwan, New Zealand, South Korea, other places. And the estimate was that if that had been applied to the whole United States, it might have saved three hundred thousand lives.[12] These are not small things.

That discontent you spoke of took a dramatic turn on January 6, with the assault on the Capitol. What was your understanding of what went on there?

First of all, it was explicitly an attempt at a coup. They were trying to overthrow the elected government. That's a coup.

The participants were a mixture. It was rather striking if you looked at the photographs, there were very few young people. That's quite unusual. Political events and demonstrations are mostly young people. This was middle-aged and older people. They were all enthusiastic Trump supporters. He was egging them on.

They all apparently fervently believe that the election was stolen, and their country is being stolen from them by evil forces. Remember, almost half of Republican voters think that Trump was sent by God to save the country from evildoers, ranging from

Democratic pedophiles, to minorities, to others who are under-mining and destroying their traditional Christian form of life.

There were elements there from the more violent militias, such as the Proud Boys. It was a pretty violent affair and came close to serious casualties among Congress and others. Five people killed. It could have been much worse. It was a desperate act by people who are desperate. We can't overlook that fact.

A large part of the country supports the assault. In fact, popularity for Trump actually increased after his instigation of the coup attempt. This is a large part of the country. If half of Republicans think that Trump was sent by God to save us from evil forces, the country is facing serious problems.

It's kind of interesting to see what happened to the Republican Party after January 6. The people who basically own the country, Adam Smith's "masters of mankind," the donor class that funds the party, they've been tolerating Trump. They don't like him. He interferes with their image of soulful, humane people. They don't like his vulgarity, his antics, but they tolerated him because he was lining their pockets. Trump's entire legislative program was designed to pour money into the pockets of the superrich and benefit the corporations—smash labor and eliminate regulations that pro tect people but interfere with profits. The whole program was that. So as long as he was doing that, they were willing to tolerate him. But January 6 was too much. And almost instantly, on January 6, the major centers of economic power, the Chamber of Commerce, Business Roundtable, and major corporate executives moved very quickly and told Trump straight out, this is enough, get lost.

Well, Trump took the plane off to Mar-a-Lago. Mitch McConnell, the most important figure in the Republican Party, heard the voice of the donors and began to sharply criticize Trump, and he and other Republican senators began to race to the exits. But they didn't go too far. Because when they reach the exits, they face the raging crowds that Trump had mobilized. So, they're stuck. And the Republican Party is stuck. Are they going to listen to the donor class and restore a more genteel version of Trumpism? Or are they going to be swept away by the forces that remain in Trump's pocket?

McConnell and Trump, the two major figures, are personally at sword points. They can't stand each other, but they have a common interest. The common interest is to ensure that the country is ungovernable and that Biden can't achieve anything. It's not a secret. It's what McConnell announced clearly and explicitly when Obama was elected.[13] At that point, McConnell didn't have Congress. He said, our task is to ensure that Obama can't succeed in doing anything. So, he cut back the stimulus that was needed and in other ways hampered efforts to govern the country and deal with the country's problems. There's every reason to suppose he'll do the same right now.

Trump wants the same thing with different goals. The two of them are combined in the effort to ensure that the country is ungovernable, that the population suffers as much as possible, in the expectation it will be blamed on the Democrats and they can come roaring back in 2022 and 2024.

The Republicans right now are kind of like the old Communist Party. They follow the principle of what the Leninists call democratic centralism. The party has a policy. It's handed down from above. Everyone uniformly must accept it. No deviation is tolerable. So even though some Republican senators and representatives may support aspects of the stimulus bill, and they know their constituents support it, they have to vote against it. That's the situation we are in now.

I must say what Biden has done so far is a rather pleasant surprise to me. It's better than I would have expected. He's pretty sharply criticized on the left for flaws and omissions in domestic policy. Foreign policy is a different issue. These criticisms are in my view correct, but a little bit unfair. There's only so much you can do when half of the Senate, no matter what you say, is going to be 100 percent opposed. And when there are Democrats who will go along with the Republicans, it puts a limit on what you can achieve.

Would you favor the elimination of the filibuster, which Barack Obama called a "Jim Crow relic"?[14]

First of all, I doubt that it can be done. So, it's basically a nonissue. Whether it should be done is another question.

The filibuster has been used in very destructive ways. But in the past, it was also used in ways to bar racist legislation. It's basically not a good idea, but it's not the fundamental issue. The basic issue is: why do we have two political parties, both of them dependent on the same narrow class of wealth and power, the donor class, basically? And one of them is so extreme that it has simply abandoned parliamentary politics. It's now fighting desperately to maintain itself as a minority party.

A lot of the major struggles underway now have to do not so much with the stimulus bills but with legislation that's passed in the House. HR1, the first legislation passed by the Democratic House, is very significant. It basically fortifies voting rights. That's critically important.

There's a major Republican assault on voting rights. There are literally hundreds of legislative proposals around the country in states where Republicans control the legislature to try to prevent minorities and poor people from voting at all, so that the Republicans can somehow maintain power. They are a minority party. They almost always lose elections. But they maintain power through various means. And this is becoming more significant. They are now in a major effort to try to cut down voting rights so that they'll be able to hang on by a thread. HR1, the Democratic proposal, calls for strengthening voting rights. The outcome of this battle will have a major effect on the future.

The Republicans have a kind of structural advantage in elections, in that the Democratic voting base is mostly concentrated in cities, which means that—given our parliamentary system—a lot of the votes are just lost. If you have 80 percent votes for a candidate in one place, it means 30 percent of them are essentially lost.

The Republican votes are scattered in rural counties, small states that have representation far beyond their population. All of this gives the Republicans a structural advantage. They can win an election, even if they lose the vote by 4 or 5 percent. And the current efforts they are undertaking are an attempt to try to sharpen and strengthen that. So, they'll be able to maintain power, even if they have even fewer votes, even if they're more of a minority party, which they're becoming for demographic reasons.

This goes along with the major McConnell project while he's been in power, to try to staff the judiciary with young, far-right lawyers who will be there at every level of the judiciary from the Supreme Court down to the lowest courts. So, they'll be in a position to bar any progressive legislation for a generation, no matter what the public may want in the years ahead.

These are all struggles going on. They're part of our highly regressive political system, which, even under the best of circumstances, would lead to a constitutional crisis. That's built in. You cannot continue to function as a formerly democratic society under the radically antidemocratic provisions of the Constitution.

The most extreme case, of course, is the Senate. The electoral college and many other things are deep problems in the whole constitutional system that can't be fixed by amendment. Smaller states won't allow it.

Talk about the potency of the canard that the election was stolen. Go back to post–World War I Germany and the stab-in-the-back theory that the Nazis used so effectively. We won the war, but communists, socialists, and Jews sabotaged us and sold us out.

I don't particularly like the word *hypocrisy*. People believed it. It wasn't hypocritical. If it was hypocritical, it wouldn't have been a problem. It's because it was not hypocritical that it's a problem. And the same in the present case. The people who say Trump won the election are not being hypocritical.

I don't know about Trump. He's off by himself. But his fervent passionate supporters clearly believe the election was stolen and their country is being stolen from them—their traditional Christian, white communities are being stolen from them. They have some basis for this. Go through a rural town in the United States. What you see are houses for sale, boarded up businesses, main street empty, the bank closed. Maybe there's still a church. The former industries are gone, young people are leaving. It's not a white Christian community anymore, where other people "knew their place." That's real.

It's the basis for the willingness to believe stories like the election was stolen, even though in fact it's the Republicans who were way in the lead in purging votes, preventing voting, making it hard for African Americans to vote. But they do fervently believe it. So, I don't think we should call it hypocrisy. It's much more dangerous than that. It's a wild belief, based on elements of reality. And that's the kind of belief that's extremely dangerous, but also offers promise, because you can deal with the elements of reality in it and let the beliefs crumble when you get rid of the elements of reality on which it's based. It's true that rural America has been smashed by neoliberal globalization. It's a fact.

That doesn't have to happen. You can overcome those facts— and with it, the belief systems will begin to erode. Not all of them, the ones that are based on white supremacy, on traditional Christian nationalism. Those are deeply embedded. Those are deep cultural problems. We're not going to deal quickly with the fact that maybe half the population, I forgot the exact numbers, expect the Second Coming to be in their lifetimes. You're not going to deal with that by solving the economic problems. But by dealing with things that are within our capacity to deal with, like the collapse of the economic base of rural communities, the destruction of poor farmers, the takeovers by agribusiness, all of these things that can be dealt with. That erodes the foundations of the very dangerous belief systems.

There's no other way to proceed. And you just have to hope that can work.

In early February, melting glaciers in the Himalayas caused floods, dams bursting, death and destruction downstream in the Indian state of Uttarakhand. In late February, a massive iceberg broke off Antarctica's Brunt Ice Shelf. At 490 square miles the iceberg is bigger than New York City, which is 302 square miles.[15]

Anybody who reads scientific journals knows that you regularly see discoveries of worse problems ahead. They're happening. What we can ask is, can we take measures to mitigate the threats and overcome the problems? And the answer to that is yes.

It's too late to stop that iceberg from pulling away from other bigger ones from going after it. That's caused by the carbon dioxide that's already in the atmosphere. The number of particles per million in the atmosphere is rising steadily into a real danger zone. And that's going to continue simply because of the damage we've done already.

It's possible that Greenland has already reached a tipping point where it may just move toward a melting stage, raising the sea level. But the question should be right before our eyes. What can we do about it? And the answer is a lot.

I talked before about the split in the Republican Party, there's a split in the Democratic Party as well—an important one. It showed up on climate policy. So, in the months leading to the primary, and then the election, I was keeping a pretty close eye on the Democratic Party website because I was giving a lot of talks and interviews, and I wanted to see what they were saying. If you looked up Democratic climate policy, what you got for a long time, into August, was Biden's program. Biden's program is not what it ought to be, but it's better than anything that came before. Thanks to the engagement of Sunrise Movement and other activists, it was not a bad program. Not enough, but not bad. In late August, it disappeared from the website.

Well, I'm not on the inside and can't be sure what happened, but I think you can make a guess. The Democratic National Committee, the Clintonite neoliberals, the Wall Street donor–oriented sector of the party, they don't want this. And I think there's going to be a real battle now as to whether Biden's program can not only be preserved but also be moved forward. And it must be moved forward if we're going to survive this.

That's the hope. The same is true on other issues. Take, say, the stimulus. The stimulus has a lot of good things on child poverty, raising incomes for the poor, and so on. But they're temporary. If they're not extended, it's not going to matter much. So, there's going to be a battle to extend them and to go beyond what they already provide.

These are major battles coming now. The Republicans apparently are just going to block everything. In the short term, there is very little hope of dislodging any of them from the attempt to render the country ungovernable and somehow get back into power, maybe by cutting back voting rights and other measures. That looks like an unstoppable force.

But within the Democrats, there's a lot that can be done, and it has to be done. We can all remember that, when Obama came into office, he came in with the enormous assistance of an army of young volunteers who worked very hard to get him elected. As soon as he got into the White House, he basically told them to go home. Thank you. Goodbye. It's all under control. Unfortunately, they went home. That meant that he could betray his promises, which he did, and within two years, he lost Congress.

If you make the same mistake today, that's what's going to happen. Whatever you think about Biden, he's going to be under pressure from the conservative sector of the Democratic Party and the Clintonite neoliberal Wall Street–oriented sector. They'll beat back progressive programs, which will be bad enough for the country—but on climate it will be disastrous.

In this pandemic/economic crisis, community efforts, mutual aid, solidarity become more important and essential. Food banks and pantries, clothing, co-ops. Talk about co-ops. Mondragon, the one in the Basque region of Spain, is often cited as a successful model.

It was a pretty interesting development that happened spontaneously in many places. People coming together in a community to provide help for one another. If there's some elderly person who can't get out, let's bring them food. If there's not enough water, let's bring water to people. Sometimes it happened in the most remarkable ways.

One of the most extraordinary examples was in the extremely poor areas in Rio de Janeiro, the favelas, which are miserable areas of horrible shacks piled on top of one another. They're basically run by criminal gangs, drug gangs, and others. If the police come in, it's like an invasion. They come in armored cars.

In the favelas, people have no water. They don't have any way to distance. They have no health care. But they did get organized. The crime gangs moved in and organized the favelas to try to help people survive these impossible conditions. And it's happened in poor areas all over.

This kind of natural commitment to mutual aid, mutual support, and solidarity revealed itself in many ways. Even before the pandemic, there was already the beginnings of the development of worker-owned industries, cooperatives, collectives, and localism in agriculture. There are many such efforts to try to deal with the extremely harmful effects of neoliberal globalization policies, which have had a real shocking effect on the general population almost everywhere.

So, in areas of the Rust Belt in the United States, where bankers in New York and Chicago had decided that the steel industry should be shifted to China, the working people didn't just give up. They tried to buy out the steel industries, but the owners wouldn't agree to it. They wanted more profit, and they don't like the idea of worker-owned industry. It's dangerous. So that was blocked. Instead, what's happened is a proliferation of worker-owned enterprises, involved in the growing service economy, hospitals, universities, and others.

Gar Alperovitz has written a lot about this and has been involved in initiating much of this work with The Next Economy project. A lot of these things have been going on. There have been moves—I don't know how far they'll go—by some of the unions, like the United Steelworkers, to enter arrangements with some of the extremely successful worker-owned conglomerates—mainly in Spain, in the Basque Country, including Mondragon—to see if something similar could be developed here.

All of those things could be very important, not only in themselves but also in showing the direction in which society must move—toward more collective responsibility, more participatory democratic activity—if we hope to emerge from these crises with any kind of a decent society.

Where you're sitting, the border with Mexico is just sixty miles away. Unaccompanied children in the thousands are being detained there. What would be a fair and just immigration policy?

The first goal of policy should be to eliminate the conditions from which they are fleeing. These people don't want to be in the United States. They want to be at home. Home is unlivable. They're forced to flee.

We have a large share of responsibility for the fact that it's unlivable. During the Reagan years, there was a sharp escalation in the US assault against Central America.[16] Hundreds of thousands of people were killed. More hundreds of thousands displaced. Torture. Destruction. People are still fleeing today from the wreckage that was created by Reagan's wars in Central America.

Well, we can deal with that wreckage. It's very, it's very easily detectable.

You may recall that the main source of refugees four or five years ago was from Honduras. Why Honduras? Because there was a military coup in Honduras, which overthrew the mildly reformist government of Manuel Zelaya, installed a military dictatorship, placed power back into the hands of the superrich oligarchy, and turned the country into one of the homicide capitals of the world.[17] People started fleeing. That's where the caravans came from. Could we have stopped it? The problem wasn't the caravans. It's the violence and repression people were fleeing.

While the whole hemisphere condemned the military coup, Obama and Hillary Clinton supported it. They refused to call it a military coup, because if they did, they would have had to stop military aid to the junta. When a fake election was run under the military regime, it was condemned all over the place. For Obama and Clinton, though, it was a positive step toward democracy. You impose a horror chamber, and people flee.

So, the first step in an immigration policy is eliminate the reasons why people are fleeing. That can't be done in a day, but you can take steps. That's the beginning. The next step is to stop the criminal policy of enlisting Mexico in preventing people from fleeing from Central America to our borders.

The only nice thing you can say about US policy is that Europe has an even worse, more cruel and sadistic policy to stop people fleeing from Africa—Niger and other places—to the territory of Europe in Turkey. Needless to say, Europe has a pretty hideous record with regard to Africa and the Middle East. We don't have to review that. So yes, they're even worse, but that doesn't excuse us. We have to put an end to that policy.

The next thing to do is to live up to the basic conditions of international law. Provide decent conditions for people fleeing, and reasonable opportunities for them to appeal for amnesty and admission. All of this can be done. It's not a huge cost.

Instead of that, what we have is thousands of people literally dying in the desert. The terrain is very forbidding. And the summer gets way over 100 degrees temperature. 120 degrees. There's no water.

Since President Clinton, the policy has been to try to drive people fleeing into the most hostile areas. So, block off the areas where there's fairly easy transit—and where, under a humane asylum policy, they could be safely picked up—and drive them into the most dangerous areas where they'll wander in the desert, get lost, and die of starvation. Meanwhile, use tactics like flying Border Patrol helicopters overhead to scatter people who are in the desert. So, if a group is together, they'll get separated, get lost, and die.

There are relief efforts. There are wonderful groups here in Tucson. The main group, No More Deaths, tries to send people into the desert to set up small encampments where they can offer some medical help if people can make it to them. They leave bottles of water in the desert for people who are dying of thirst. The Border Patrol breaks into the camps, destroys water bottles, and so on.

Before Trump, there was kind of a tacit agreement that the activists and Border Patrol would leave each other alone. But this has gotten much worse. All these horror stories don't have to happen. The several layers in which policies have to be shaped are completely feasible.

The murder of George Floyd triggered widespread protests across the United States and even around the world. Some have called this a moment of racial reckoning. Terms like white supremacy, white privilege, and systemic racism are much more commonplace than ever before. Where do you see the racial justice movement going?

The upsurge after the George Floyd murder was impressive. It didn't happen all at once. It's the result of years of organizing, education, and activism that laid a basis so that when this spark came, the kindling could burn. And it was an amazing uprising. Solidarity. Black and white together.

The uprising had enormous popular support, about two-thirds popular support, which is almost unknown for a social movement. Take a look at Martin Luther King. He never came close to that, even at the peak of his popularity.

A lot of it is maintained. Some has dissipated, partly because of tactical errors, failures of one kind or another that you should pay attention to. The slogan "Defund the police" became prominent very quickly. It's a sensible idea and it has a very sensible interpretation. It was given by Black Lives Matter organizers, Bernie Sanders, Ocasio-Cortez, and others. The meaning of it is let's remove the police from activities where they don't belong. The police have no role in domestic disputes, overdoses, suicide attempts, things like that. All those issues should involve community service organizations. They can handle them properly. Leave the police to do police work.

Actually, Ocasio-Cortez was asked once, what do you mean by defund the police? And her answer was, go to a white suburban community—that's what I mean by defund the police.[18] If a kid is caught breaking a window to steal drugs, you don't send him to jail for thirty years. What you do is find out what his problem is and deal with it. Okay, that's defund the police. But the slogan was hijacked by the right wing. And it became a propaganda story about "Look at these crazy lunatics." They want to remove all the police from communities so that you'll be subjected to terrorists, criminals, and rapists. Well, nobody wants that. It was a big talking point for the right wing and the Trump campaign.

There's a lesson. We have to be careful how to back up your proposals with meaningful educational, organizational, and activist programs to say, here's what I mean. It's a good idea. It's good for you, you should support it. Don't fall for the propaganda line that's coming. That was a failure.

There were other things, but basically, it's a major step forward. And I think you can build on it. It's not the only example. The 1619 Project in the *New York Times* was another very interesting step forward. Of course, it's being lambasted by professional historians. You got this detail wrong, forgot to say that. It doesn't matter. It was a very powerful recognition of what four hundred years of vicious treatment has meant for African Americans and what legacy it leaves. That's a real breakthrough. A couple of years earlier, there was nothing like it. All of these are steps forward.

#MeToo has brought long overdue attention to sexual harassment, discrimination, and violence toward women. This is a major development, culturally, socially, in the United States.

Not only in the United States. It's also taking place elsewhere. It's long overdue. It's good that it's being recognized that steps have to be taken to overcome this.

You conclude the chapter on social change in *Consequences of Capitalism* with Karl Marx's "old mole."[19]

Karl Marx had this image of a revolutionary spirit, which is just below the surface. Going back to David Hume, where we began, power is based on consent. But beneath that consent, there is a current of people saying, I don't really want this. I don't want to be ruled by a master. And it doesn't take much for that to break through. And when it does, you have the kinds of changes that really make a society move forward.

So, that old mole is burrowing in there. And it can go in many ways.

I think Marx's old mole is right beneath the surface. If there's an opportunity to think about it, to recognize the possibility that you don't have to be subject to a master, you can run your own life, you can run your own enterprises, that keeps coming very close to the surface. The sit-down strikes when I was a child during the Depression, they were a step toward saying, we don't need the bosses, we can take this place over and run it ourselves, which is true.

That's when attitudes changed and support for New Deal measures really grew across the population. That's when the Supreme

Court stopped blocking all New Deal measures, when sectors of capital recognized, Look, we've got to accommodate ourselves to these rising developments, or else we'll be in real trouble.

And I think this keeps coming out. The New Economy project that I mentioned is moving in that direction to saying you can run your own enterprises. It doesn't have to be bankers in New York who decide whether this enterprise moves to China. You can decide how you want to run it.

You can decide in solidarity with workers in China and Mexico, making life better for all of you. You have common interests.

Many unions have the word *international* in their names. The names usually don't mean much. But it can mean a lot and can be brought to the surface.

And it's quite striking at this moment. We're in a period where internationalism is in the forefront. The pandemic, global warming—these are international issues. Addressing them has to be done together. You can't do it in one place alone. You can't stop global warming in the West. The pandemic has no borders. Labor rights have no borders. The repression of labor in China and Mexico harms workers in the United States.

We can work together on this. That's the direction things should move.

Did you get your vaccine?

I got the second one two days ago. I have a bit of a sore arm.

How are you dealing with the isolation?

For other people, it's very difficult. But it's easy for us. We can stay alone.

THE UNITED STATES RULES THE WORLD

Oro Valley, Arizona   June 21, 2021

The pandemic is raging in some parts of the world and waning in others. Rajan Menon writes, "Finally, a return to normalcy seems likely for a distinct minority of the world's people, those living mainly in the United States, Canada, the United Kingdom, the European Union, and China. That's not surprising. The concentration of wealth and power globally has enabled rich countries to all but monopolize available vaccine doses. For the citizens of low-income and poor countries to have long-term pandemic security, especially the 46% of the world's population who survive on less than $5.50 a day, this inequity must end, rapidly—but don't hold your breath."[1]

The rich countries—the United States, Canada, and Europe—have essentially monopolized the vaccine. They have more doses than they can use. They even have a reserve for the future.

Meanwhile, in India and the rest of South Asia, Africa, and Latin America, there is a severe shortage of vaccines.

There is an international organization, COVAX, which is supposed to be concerned with this distributional equity ensuring that the countries who need the vaccine can get it. We discussed the fact that most countries are members of the organization. Trump pulled out of it, of course, but Biden rejoined. In fact,

149

they're doing very little to deal with the desperate need for vaccines in much of the world.

This is not only deeply immoral, but it's also suicidal. And they know it. They know that if these poor countries do not quickly get vaccines, there will be mutations, like the Delta mutation. There will be others. Some of these mutations may be uncontrollable. But the attitude of working for ourselves, not helping anyone else, is so extreme that it even leads to suicidal behavior, like letting mutants develop, which will, of course come back and harm us.

In addition, there's the effort on the part of a number of rich countries to guarantee patent rights over the product and the process of manufacturing the product. So, of course, that guarantees exorbitant profits and restricts availability.

There are efforts to construct what's called a people's vaccine. Just free up the information about the product and the process of manufacturing. That would, of course, allow India, South Africa, and other countries to develop their own approaches. It would expedite the rapid control of the disease. But there's very limited support for that. It's an indication that we are facing a world in which we will either cooperate or go extinct. That's putting it strongly, but not too strongly.

The problems we face have no borders. That's obviously true of the pandemic, obviously true of global warming, and also true of nuclear weapons. If there's a nuclear war anywhere, that affects everyone.

We are in a situation where we either move toward the kind of internationalism Cuba has exhibited in its response to the pandemic or we will go down together.

Didn't the Biden administration offer several million doses to different countries?

Early on, the Biden administration offered the AstraZeneca vaccine, which had not been approved by the Food and Drug Administration.[2] So it was in storage. And of course, it stays in storage, its shelf life ends soon. Biden did offer these vaccines, which couldn't be used in the United States, to other countries. The other countries were Canada, which probably has more stored vaccines than any other, and Mexico, where it was offered as a bribe, essentially, to try to get Mexico to agree to the illegal US efforts to block asylum seekers. The Biden administration wants Mexico to cooperate by keeping them from our borders. So, vaccines were given to them.

More recently, Biden has offered more vaccines more broadly. It's not very clear to whom and where, but at least this is a small step forward.

A relatively new term has come up in Washington. I'd like you to translate it please into plain English, and that is "a rules-based international order."

In plain English, it means, "Do what we say or else." We make the rules. If we don't like the rules, we throw them out. But we want you to observe the rules we establish. You'd better do it, or else you're in trouble.

The United States doesn't pay any attention to most rules. The United States just doesn't ratify most laws and international conventions.

What about the International Criminal Court? The US did sign it but then did not ratify it.

Correct. It was never ratified. So the United States is technically not a member. However, the United States has acted severely, just to block the ICC from doing things that Washington doesn't like, even imposed sanctions. In fact, as you may recall, under the George W. Bush administration, legislation was passed that Europeans call the Netherlands Invasion Act. It's an act that grants the US executive, the president, the right to use military force to rescue any US citizen who is brought to The Hague for trial by any international tribunal. The United States is alone in this.

The United States has avoided international jurisdiction in other interesting ways. So, Yugoslavia brought a case to the World Court, charging NATO with abuses in its bombing of Yugoslavia. The other NATO powers accepted the jurisdiction. Of course, the case was thrown out later. But they accepted. Not the United States—which excused itself. And the World Court accepted the excuse. The excuse was that the Yugoslav appeal case had mentioned genocide. And the United States is self-exempted from the Genocide Convention.

The United States didn't pay attention to the Genocide Convention for, I think, about forty years. But then the United States finally did sign it—however, with the reservation: excluding the United States. So, therefore, the United States formally claims that it has the right to commit genocide. And on those grounds, it was exempted from the World Court hearings on the bombing of Serbia.

What did you think of the Biden administration's acknowledgment of the Armenian Genocide?

There was a lot of pressure to do that. It's been languishing in Congress for a long time. I don't know exactly what led to it now. But, yes, they finally did recognize the Armenian Genocide during the First World War. It's not hard for the United States to do, because it's somebody else's crime. There's no recognition of the extermination of Native Americans, for example.

Given the level of rhetoric, sanctions, military maneuvers from Washington toward Beijing, are we heading into a new Cold War? Maybe I should change the tense and ask if we are in a new Cold War?

So far, it's a one-sided new Cold War. The Trump administration had been fairly aggressive toward China. The Biden administration has escalated tensions. It's bipartisan. The Republicans love it. The military industry is practically salivating with joy over the new militant steps, which offer them a great deal. The Democrats are supporting it.

It's a bipartisan campaign that is not only idiotic but extremely hazardous. Look at the timeline of actions that's been taken. It's shocking. Just building up a "yellow peril" hysteria, which of course goes way back to the 1880s, when Chinese were barred from entry to the United States. It picked up again in the 1950s with lunacy about Chinese threats to conquer and destroy the United States. This has been so extreme that it's even reached what are called progressive circles. Like, early in the twentieth century, Jack London, a progressive writer, wrote a story called "The Unparalleled Invasion."[3] It's about how the United States should carry out bacteriological warfare and wipe out the Chinese to prevent them from attacking us.

Now it's being revived. And to the extent to which it's being revived—if it wasn't so serious, you'd call it comical. So Chuck Schumer wants to push through what's called an infrastructure bill, something the United States desperately needs given its collapsing infrastructure. And the bill includes other measures like improving our collapsing educational system, providing some limited form of childcare, as they have in just about every other developed country. In order to do these things that are essential for the United States, it had to be put in the framework of an anti-China bill saying we have to make sure that China doesn't get ahead of us in artificial intelligence or semiconductors or whatever else. And in order to make sure that China doesn't get ahead of us, let's do what's essential for our needs. We can't get it through otherwise.

Of course, if it had been done without the "hate China" part, Republicans would have been 100 percent opposed. As long as it's in the framework of more militarism, more violence, more threats of war, and "hate China" racism, then the Republicans are willing to come on board enthusiastically—and the Democrats, too. It's madness.

If you look at what's actually happening on the ground, it's un-believable. Chinese bombers have actually penetrated Taiwanese air defenses. Meanwhile, Biden sends a huge naval armada with two major aircraft carriers into the South China Sea. These are highly provocative measures that could explode at any time. And notice, it's not in the Caribbean—it's in the South China Sea.

Actually, China is doing things in the South China Sea that it shouldn't be doing. It is violating international law. But the United States is hardly in a strong position to complain about that, since the United States is the one country that has not even accepted the rule of international law, the Law of the Sea. So what kind of standing do we have to criticize China in its own regional area? The South China Sea is of extraordinary strategic and commercial significance for China. It's their one avenue to the rest of the world.

China, of course, is contained, as we put it, by US nuclear bases and allies. There's a ring surrounding China from the east, Guam, other Pacific Islands, Okinawa, Korea, US nuclear forces. Take a look at a map. The ring essentially blocks off China from the Pacific. Their one more or less free avenue is through the South China Sea, which has to go through the narrow Straits of Malacca, controlled by US allies. All of this doesn't justify Chi-nese actions in the South China Sea, but it goes a long way toward explaining them.

The United States is now strengthening what's called the QUAD, the Quadrilateral Security Dialogue, an anti-Chinese alliance of India, Australia, Japan, and the United States. Japan has a very right-wing government. Australia has a far-right gov-ernment. India is under an extremist, right-wing government. All three are joining with the United States to defend the freedom of the seas, and defend the rule of law. If it wasn't so ominous, you'd burst out laughing. But it is very ominous. We have to pre-vent Chinese development. We have to prevent their commer-cial expansion. We have to do everything to ensure that there's no possible challenge to US global dominance. We're concerned about the Chinese military.

China's military expenditures are a tiny fraction of ours. We spend about 40 percent, I think, and the Chinese spend about 15 percent, if you look at the latest figures of global armaments expenditures.[4] They're in a far more vulnerable position than we are. They're surrounded by enemies.

Per capita, of course, China's military spending is far less. But we have to be concerned that they might overwhelm us. It's sanction after sanction. Even the politicization of the COVID-19 origins issue, which is framed as an anti-China campaign, not as a campaign to try to figure out what happened because maybe we can all work together to help ourselves. The madness that is developing in the United States over this is shocking but unfortunately familiar. As I said, it goes back to the 1880s.

Talk about some of China's internal issues, its oppression of the Uyghur Muslim minority in western China, Tibet, Hong Kong, worker unrest. At the same time, there's a class of billionaires that's exploded in China.

There are abuses that should be condemned.

Chinese capitalism is probably even more unequal than American capitalism—certainly comparable. It's a very unequal society.

I don't think anything new has happened in Tibet. It's an old problem. In Hong Kong, China has become more repressive, imposing restrictions on Hong Kong's democracy, which, we should recall, is a recent democracy. Hong Kong was a British colony, stolen from China by violence during the period when Britain was leading the global war against China.

The Chinese don't forget this. We might forget it. But in the nineteenth century, we might recall that a large part of the basis for the wealth of Britain and its offshoots was narcotrafficking. It was a major enterprise. Britain conquered much of India to gain a monopoly of the opium trade, which it could then use to force opium into China at gunpoint.

China had been the richest and most advanced country in the world. But Europe was far superior in the means of savagery and violence. That's how Europe conquered the world. There are abuses that should be condemned.

When the Chinese administrator in Canton province approached Queen Victoria to ask her to enforce the law and prevent British narcotraffickers from violating the privileges granted to them in Canton, Queen Victoria responded by sending the British navy to destroy China's fleet and its defenses and force more opium into China. The British then invaded, even conquered Beijing, destroyed the Summer Palace. All of this for narcotrafficking. Part of it was stealing Hong Kong, turning it into a base for the British narcotrafficking empire.

Actually, the Americans were involved in this too. You look at the wealthy families in the United States and the concentration of wealth. Many of them go back to participation in the narcotrafficking racket of the nineteenth century. I think opium for a time was the major commodity in world trade. The most famous of the wealthy Americans was Franklin Delano Roosevelt. His grandfather Warren Delano made a killing in the China trade by narcotrafficking. He left a huge legacy to the Delano family including Franklin Delano Roosevelt, who believed that he had special insight into China because of the stories his mother, Sara Delano, told him about the exploits of his grandfather. That led to very severe consequences, I should say.

All of this is a large part of the background about Hong Kong. It doesn't excuse what China's doing. But again, it's worth understanding the context.

With regard to Xinjiang region and the Uyghurs, there are very credible reports of severe human rights abuses. Amnesty International, Human Rights Watch, a couple of others, report about apparently a million people have been sent through reeducation camps.[5] And some were treated extremely harshly. That should be condemned, along with many other things.

So, for example, take the two million people, half of them children, imprisoned in Gaza with US aid. They are subject to far harsher treatment than anything that's credibly been reported about the Uyghurs. And while we can't do much about the Uyghur abuses, except to condemn them, we can do a great deal about the evidently far worse abuses that we are helping to implement in Gaza. But we don't talk about that.

That invokes my late friend Ed Herman's terminology. There are what he called "worthy and unworthy victims."[6] The worthy victims are victims of some official enemy, which we can't do much about. The unworthy victims are the ones we can do a great deal about because we are responsible for the abuse. So, we focus on the worthy victims and ignore the unworthy ones.

China is on track to become the world's largest economy in a very few years. What are the implications of that?

China is the world's largest economy if you use purchasing power parity as one of the measures. It doesn't mean much. In the eighteenth century, China was the world's largest economy. Did that protect them from European and American savagery?

First of all, look at the measures per capita. Of course, if you have a bigger population, you have a larger economy. China has almost five times the population of the United States. So, in per capita terms, it's way below. Look at the Human Development Index of the United Nations, which is a measure attempting to include various factors in human development. Last time I looked China was, I think, about ninetieth.[7] It's a relatively poor country, which has major internal problems. It has enormous ecological problems, demographic problems. It is a brutally authoritarian state that imposes harsh conditions.

China has made unprecedented gains in economic development in recent years, with many achievements before that. So, it's often forgotten, or maybe overlooked, that during the Maoist years, roughly 1949 to 1979, China saved 100 million lives as compared with India during the same years.[8] These are comparable cases of societies trying to develop. India killed 100 million people as compared with China, just because it didn't implement rural development programs—health, education, support for development—that were undertaken in China in the Maoist years. One hundred million is not a small number. That, incidentally, includes deaths from the Chinese famine. Even with that, 100 million saved. That laid part of the basis for Chinese later development.

It's a very mixed story. China has enormous problems. It's way behind the West in development. It has problems unknown in Western societies. The idea that we should be trying to impede Chinese development because it might someday compete with us is—I just can't find words for it. I mean, we should be cooperating with them for the common good.

We should be condemning their crimes. They should be condemning our crimes. We should be condemning our crimes and doing something about them—not just condemning.

You're saying the Indian 100 million deaths were due to poverty?

It was due to the failure to undertake the rural reforms that were undertaken under Mao. Health programs, education programs, help for rural development. This wasn't done under Indian state capitalism.

There's a very interesting story about this. This traces back to work by Amartya Sen, a Nobel laureate and a highly regarded economist and specialist on India. He had an article in the journal of the American Academy of Arts and Sciences in which he discussed the Chinese famine and compared India to China.[9] Half of the article has been read—the part on the Chinese famine, which of course you can condemn. The other half of the article disappeared. Sen later did a more extensive study with Jean

Drèze, a well-known Indian economist, in a book in which they went through the details on this.[10] I've never seen a mention of it except for what I've written a couple of times.

One hundred million is an interesting number. There was, as you may recall, a publication called *The Black Book of Communism*.[11] It was widely publicized, with rave reviews all over the place, despite rather dubious empirical evidence. It claimed that the communist powers, mostly China, were responsible for 100 million deaths. So, 100 million is quite a famous number. As I say, the empirical basis of this book is pretty weak. But for the sake of argument, let's say it's true. What about the fact that China saved 100 million people as compared with India? Unmentioned. This finding is backed by US government statistics on demographic growth. This continued until 1979. After that, the demographic improvements declined as China moved into the state capitalist mode.

It's also worth remembering that Mao tried very hard in the 1940s to approach American emissaries to propose an accord between China and the United States, which is very much like what developed in the last period, with China providing huge manpower while the United States would provide capital. That was Mao's proposal in the late 1940s, totally dismissed throughout the 1940s. The United States insisted on supporting the quasi-fascist Chiang Kai-shek regime, which didn't want to fight the Japanese. Money was poured into Chiang's pocket. He enriched himself and the Soong family. But it wasn't being used to fight the Japanese invaders.

It was Mao's peasant army, off in the northwest, that was fighting the Japanese. Mao wanted to cooperate with Chiang. Chiang wouldn't do it. He wanted to save the huge military resources being poured in for a war against Mao, after the Japanese were driven out by the Americans. It's very similar to what happened in Vietnam, when Ho Chi Minh was pleading for US support and cooperation during the same years. By 1950, after China liberated itself, the United States wouldn't hear it.

So, these are very important stories which should be well known. They are known to the Chinese, of course. They should be known to us.

Again, this doesn't excuse Chinese crimes, which are serious, but it helps explain them. We should be interested in understanding the history from which these things are developing.

Talk about China's Belt and Road Initiative. The Council on Foreign Relations, an establishment organization, says of it, "China's colossal infrastructure investments may usher in a new era of trade and growth for economies in Asia and beyond." Then adds, "But skeptics worry that China is laying a debt trap for borrowing governments."[12]

The Belt and Road Initiative grew out of what's called the Shanghai Cooperation Organization, which was established some years ago by China. It includes the Central Asian states, Russia, Pakistan, and India. They excluded the United States, which asked for observer status but was rejected. So it's a China-based development initiative through Central Asia, including Pakistan, reaching in principle as far as Turkey, and thereby entering the European market.

The Belt and Road Initiative is an expansion of this, with lots of infrastructure development. You can take a high-speed train from Beijing to Kazakhstan, but you can't take one from New York to Washington. The United States is in some respects a third world country. Fortunately, in the framework of hating China, maybe we can develop something. This, of course, links together. There's a lot of Chinese development in Pakistan. There's a major port at Gwadar on the Arabian Sea that would give China access to Africa and Europe.

China's loans have punitive elements like everybody's loans, but they don't seem to be out of the normal range in that respect. They're not like International Monetary Fund loans, which have conditionalities requiring countries to impose destructive structural adjustment programs. They're free of those condition-alities. I'm sure there are negative aspects to them, but they don't look the least out of the ordinary. If it succeeds, the Belt and Road Initiative will integrate Central Asia—ultimately, extending to Europe and Africa—within a Chinese dominated system.

The US is trying very hard to stop this all over the place, even in Israel. So, for example, Israel put out a tender for the develop-ment of a light rail system. And a couple of Chinese firms applied for it. They very likely would have gotten the offer. But the United States is intervening hard to try to prevent Israel from allowing China to carry out development projects in Israel. China already administers the Haifa port, which the United States doesn't like at all. It's a major US naval base.

That's just an example. But all over the world, the same thing is happening. You saw what happened in one of the last acts of the Trump administration: to pressure Panama to expel Cuban doc-tors, because we don't want the malign influence of Cuba to help out Panama in the midst of the COVID-19 crisis.[13]

Same kind of pressures to keep countries from using the Chinese vaccines. Brazil is very short of vaccines because of Bol-sonaro's criminality. Brazil is in a major crisis. The United States has been pressuring all along not to use Chinese vaccines, which are in fact manufactured in Brazil, and not to use Russian vac-cines, which are, according to Western sources, about the same as Western vaccines.

We have to make sure that the United States rules the world. To go back to your first question about the rule of law, that's the rule. The US rules the world—and any move to modify that, no matter how benign, is unacceptable. It's not anything the United States invented. Britain was the same during its period of global hegemony. France is the same in the regions it dominates. Russia is the same in the much smaller regions it dominates.

Talk about US relations with Russia and how they've evolved.

There was an amusing column by conservative columnist Ross Douthat in the *New York Times* asking why liberals are backing off from Russophobia.[14] The fact is that Trump had carried out quite provocative actions with regard to Russia, just as Obama had. And it seems to be increasing under the Biden administration.

Quite generally, Biden's foreign policy team has been more aggressive than even Trump's. That's not entirely true. Biden came into office just in time to salvage the New START Treaty, which was going to expire in February. Trump had refused Russian offers to extend it. Biden accepted them. That was a good step. Apart from that, the United States has been mostly increasing tensions. There are plenty of areas of serious contention. But what's needed is diplomacy, negotiation, working out problems peacefully, not increasing provocation, which is not only wrong but basically suicidal. If something moves on to a real conflict, we're in serious trouble. All of us. In fact, we're finished.

A new international issue is cyberwarfare. Iran gets attacked. Iran counterattacks. Russia attacks, the US counterattacks. This could have potentially serious consequences.

According to the Pentagon, cyberwar is comparable to a military attack—and it justifies a military response. There is, so far, one very successful example of effective cyberwar, namely, the US attack on Iran's nuclear development system and destruction of the equipment involved in nuclear power production under Obama. The United States managed to destroy it with a major cyberattack, and took pride in that. It wasn't secret, it was regarded as a great achievement.

As I say, according to Pentagon standards, Iran would have been entitled to launch a military attack in response. Of course, that's out of the question. So, it's kind of like the worthy and unworthy victims story. When we do it, no matter how destructive it is, it's praiseworthy. We don't hide it.

But it is a danger. Others might use cyber warfare the way we do. And there is now a US Cyber Command, which is working on ways of blocking cyberwar attacks. I'm sure other countries are doing the same thing. It's another area where treaty agreements would protect everyone. You can't prevent rogue elements, but you can at least control states. And that would make a big difference. But that's not on the agenda, apparently—only escalating conflict.

Eisenhower, no dove, in a 1953 speech, talked about "the cloud of threatening war, it is humanity hanging from a cross of iron."[15] You've mentioned the Damocles sword that hangs over humanity and the planet. What is the state of the various arms agreements? Biden has not rejoined the Open Skies Treaty.

The Open Skies Treaty was initiated during the Eisenhower period and enacted later. It's a very important treaty that reduces tensions by permitting surveillance of Russia and the United States. Each can carry out surveillance of the other, recognize what's happening to prevent false alarms—and there have been many false alarms. It doesn't have quite the status that it did sixty years ago because of advances in satellites and so on, but it's an important treaty.

Trump revoked it, just as he revoked every treaty he could. Biden has not rejoined it, nor has he made any move to rejoin the Intermediate-Range Nuclear Forces Treaty, which significantly reduced the threat of conflict in Europe, which could have easily broken out. He's done nothing on that. He has also done nothing on the Iran agreement, the Joint Comprehensive Plan of Action, contrary to what's constantly claimed. Biden simply took over the Trump policy.

Trump withdrew from the Iran agreement, over the very strong objections of all other participants. Biden has made some rhetorical changes, but in practice he's accepted the whole Trump program. The sanctions remain. It's Iran that is sanctioned after the United States withdrew from the agreement. It's the United States that sanctions. The sanctions are over the objection of the

Europeans. They don't agree with them, but they have to accept them. They have to adhere to them under US threat.

It's very interesting what's happening now. The *New York Times* had a very interesting editorial a couple of days ago. They called for a nuclear weapons–free zone in the Middle East.[16] Actually, that's been the right idea for decades. We've talked about it. I've been talking about it constantly. There should be a nuclear weapons–free zone in the Middle East. A nuclear weapons–free zone with inspections would end any possible threat, whether you believe the threats or not, real or imagined, about Iranian nuclear weapons. So, it's interesting that the *New York Times* suggested it—with a proviso that it exclude Israel. That it would exclude the one nuclear state in the region, of course, kills it. A proper nuclear weapons–free zone would include the states of the region, including the one state that has a massive nuclear weapons capacity. But the *Times* editors carefully excised that part.

In fact, that's the reason why the United States, alone, has been vetoing a nuclear weapons–free zone for years, which the *Times* editors failed to mention. Obama vetoed it because it would include Israel. The Arab states are in favor of it. Iran's in favor of it. The Global South is in favor of it, strongly. Europe's in favor of it. The United States vetoes.

As we've discussed before—it's crucial, so I'll repeat it—the United States does not recognize that Israel has nuclear weapons. That would immediately raise questions about US law, which bans aid to countries that are developing nuclear weapons outside the framework of international agreements. Neither political party in the United States has wanted to open that door. Activists haven't pursued it, but they should.

So, here's an opening. The *New York Times* calls for a nuclear weapons–free zone, excluding the one nuclear weapon state in the region. Fine. Let's work for extending it, which ends any imagined Iranian threat and the need for sanctions, and we move toward a more peaceful world without serious threat of conflict, escalating conflict. A perfect solution. But instead you have to support illegal US aid to Israel.

A researcher for the Nobel Prize–winning International Campaign to Abolish Nuclear Weapons says that "despite Biden's campaign promises of wanting to work for arms control, wanting to work for disarmament, we're seeing that in reality he's going full steam ahead with Trump's legacy nuclear weapons programs and continuing to spend more money on these weapons of mass destruction."[17] Why, during a pandemic, with people dying in large numbers, is the United States modernizing its nuclear weapons arsenal?

Two reasons. One is called money. The money is not thrown into the ocean. Money for weapons development goes into the pockets of the arms manufacturers. And that's not just military industry. A large swath of American industry is involved in one way or another in arms production, indirectly in many ways.

Furthermore, Congress wants it for lots of crazy reasons. So, the Pentagon has been careful to scatter Minuteman emplacements in rural areas in states like North Dakota, where they become small commercial centers. This is a part of the arms system that in fact harms the United States. Every strategic analyst knows that the Minuteman has no utility as a deterrent. What it does is attract attack. These are fixed emplacements. Russia knows where they are. China knows where they are. If there's any threat of war, the first thing they'll do is attack them to take them out of commission. Let's face it. They serve no purpose. They add nothing to military capacity. But even at the point of direct harm to ourselves, it's necessary to increase arms.

Actually, the same is true of the expanded nuclear weapons system that simply leads to greater threats, greater tension. Hypersonic missiles, weaponizing outer space—these are all increasing the threat to us for two purposes. One, the money goes to centers of private capital. Two, it enhances the appearance of US domination of the world. We can always, as every president says, outspend them. We can waste more money than they can waste because we have a richer economy. So instead of using resources to deal with our scandalous health system, collapsing infrastructure, declining educational system, and minimal social welfare, let's develop an outer space command so we have better ways of killing ourselves and everyone else. Basically, that's what it amounts to.

The United Nations treaty for the prevention of nuclear weapons production went into force a couple of months ago, to block any development of nuclear weapons. It was signed by 122 countries. None of the nuclear states signed.[18] But the Biden administration could take steps to induce other nuclear states to move toward accepting the basic provisions of this new treaty. That would mean accepting our obligation under the Non-Proliferation Treaty to make good faith efforts to eliminate nuclear weapons. All of that is perfectly possible—and, with enough public pressure, it could happen.

Just like establishing nuclear weapons–free zones, it could happen. As we've discussed, it's not just the Middle East zone. That's the most important, but there are others. What about the Africa zone? There is an Africa nuclear weapons–free zone, but it can't be implemented because the British reject international law and international judgments to maintain their former colonial possession of Diego Garcia. They expelled most of the population of the island to allow the United States to establish a military base there, which was upgraded to a nuclear military base under Obama. So that prevents the implementation of the African nuclear weapons–free zone.

Diego Garcia is not just symbolic. It's a base used for the bombing of Central Asia and the Middle East.

The same is true in the Pacific. There is a Pacific nuclear weapons–free zone, but it's blocked by US insistence on maintaining nuclear facilities on certain islands.

Which islands are those?

Guam is one. Technically, the United States is not supposed to have nuclear weapons in Japan. But there's been case after case where it's been exposed that there are nuclear weapons on US ships in Japanese harbors.

Kashmir is an unresolved issue of the 1947 British partition of the Indian subcontinent. The desires of the people of the Indian-occupied area were largely ignored; New Delhi never followed through on a plebiscite. In 1989, an uprising began and has continued on and off since. Thousands have been killed, many have disappeared. The Indian-occupied area might be the most densely militarized zone on Earth. Arundhati Roy has written extensively about Kashmir in her book *Azadi*, meaning freedom, and elsewhere.[19] Sanjay Kak is a Kashmiri. He is a renowned documentary filmmaker and editor of an extraordinary book on Kashmir called *Witness*.[20] In August 2019, the BJP-led Hindu nationalist government under Narendra Modi annulled Article 370 of India's constitution. This was the last vestige of the terms under which the former princely state of Jammu and Kashmir had acceded to India in 1947. It was rammed through parliament and came with an unprecedented clampdown by the military and paramilitary forces, and the longest internet shutdown by any democracy. It gave birth to the term "digital apartheid."[21] Despite the welcome coverage in the US media of what's happened in Kashmir recently, and of the disastrous handling of the pandemic all across India, the Biden administration continues to turn a blind eye to the dismantling of India's democratic pretensions.

In other words, the norm. It's a horror story. What Modi's done in Kashmir is totally outrageous. In fact, Indian behavior in Kashmir has been criminal ever since the fraudulent elections in the late 1980s. Kashmir has been one of the most militarized areas in the world. Deeply oppressive Indian actions escalated under Modi and, of course, the United States keeps a blind eye.

Kashmir is occupied. Palestine is occupied. Western Sahara is occupied. The occupation of Western Sahara by Morocco was authorized by Trump, just as he authorized the Israeli annexation of the Syrian Golan Heights.

The Abraham Accords, which were greatly applauded in the United States, are quite interesting. The accords are between the most reactionary states in the region, the Gulf dictatorships, where Mohammed bin Salman, the crown prince of Saudi Arabia, has been given a mark of approval by the Biden administration for his criminal atrocities. The Sisi government, the most brutal government in Egypt's history, is a partner. The Gulf dictatorships may be the most reactionary states in the world. Israel, which has moved very far to the right, provides the muscle.

And they brought in Morocco. Morocco is a member of the Abraham Accords, which is interesting. Of course, it's another dictatorship. But why Morocco? Because one element of the Abraham Accords is to take control of the major resources of the region. In the Gulf dictatorships, the resource is oil. What about Morocco? Morocco has a virtual monopoly over phosphates, which are essential for agriculture. Western Sahara also has phosphates. That's the main reason why Morocco wants to take it over.

Trump authorized that as another way to guarantee that the reactionary alliance controlled by Washington, which also includes Modi's India, will also dominate the resources of the region. That's the main geostrategic program of the Trump administration, adopted also by Biden.

Archbishop Desmond Tutu says, "If you are neutral in situations of injustice, you have chosen the side of the oppressor."[22] Talk about your commitment to justice and what you've accomplished over the years, not just in terms of your scholarship but also inspiring so many people.

That's for other people to answer, not me. I've done what I can. It's for others to judge its validity and its efficacy.

Howard Zinn closes his masterwork, *A People's History of the United States*, with a poem by Percy Shelley, "The Masque of Anarchy":

> Rise like lions after slumber
> in unvanquishable number!
> Shake your chains to earth, like dew
> Which in sleep had fallen on you:
> Ye are many—they are few.

That's how the book concludes: "Ye are many—they are few."[23]

That's always been true. You can take it back to my favorite philosopher, David Hume. As long as people consent and accept and subordinate themselves, the few will be able to rule the many, no matter how much they harm them. When the many recognize their own power and rise up, they can change things.

TIPPING POINTS:
ENVIRONMENTAL AND POLITICAL

Oro Valley, Arizona   September 30, 2021

In the United States, COVID-19 has resulted in more than seven hundred thousand deaths, exceeding the 1918 pandemic figure. Globally, the death toll is in the millions. We'll probably never know the exact number. There's the Delta variant now. And we're all wondering, will there be other variants? Vaccines have been effective, yet there's a significant resistance to vaccinations, particularly in the United States. Why? There are bizarre notions of freedom and individual rights. "No one is going to tell me what to do!" But if there aren't universal vaccinations, we won't get past this pandemic. In Africa, for example, only 4 percent of the continent's population has been fully vaccinated.[1] What makes some people susceptible to conspiracy theories about getting vaccinated?

If you look at global maps, the United States stands out. It's the main global hotspot outside of Mongolia and a couple of other countries. If you look closely, it's not the United States. It's selected parts of the United States. Overwhelmingly, it's the old Confederacy and a couple of outliers like Idaho and Wyoming, which are rock-ribbed Republican states. There's even been

171

analysis by counties by now, and it turns out that there's a quite sharp difference between counties that voted for Biden and counties that voted for Trump.[2] So, to a very substantial extent, it's a partisan issue.

Parts of the left have bought into vaccine conspiracies, too. They're not, I don't think, statistically significant as compared with the mass refusal on the part of Republicans, but it's very serious. COVID is killing hundreds of thousands of people. It's also endangering many others. The hospitals in Republican areas like Idaho and Alabama are being crushed by cases. Hospitals have stopped providing regular services because they have no place. Actually, that happened to me, too. I couldn't get to a hospital that I needed to because they had no beds. It was a minor issue. I survived.

The unvaccinated are endangering others. They're severely endangering children, who can't get vaccinated yet. They have no protection. They're even endangering the vaccinated. I mean, the vaccine is very effective, but not 100 percent. And on top of that, they're creating a pool in which the virus can mutate freely, maybe leading to variants that might not be treatable. It could be a raging untreatable pandemic.

Why is this done? Liberty? There's no such liberty. There's no liberty that allows you to drive through a red light because you feel like it, and you don't want to be inhibited. Nobody's ever claimed such a liberty. It's outlandish. You want to hurt people? Okay, go find a plot of land somewhere, sit on it, don't take any benefits from the government, and don't take any responsibilities. There's no liberty involved. The whole libertarian position is pure nonsense.

Furthermore, we've had vaccine mandates, strict ones. Much stricter than now, for years. You can't send your kid to school without a vaccine, rightly. Why should you be able to endanger other children? So, that's been in place for a long time.

There are no real vaccine mandates now. What's called mandates have an alternative. You can agree to get tested every week or two. This is, I think, a symptom of severe social disorder and the social collapse of a former political party that has simply gone rogue. That's not just my opinion. A day or two ago, the *Financial Times*, the major business newspaper in the world, sober, conservative, their leading correspondent, Martin Wolf—a highly respected, conservative analyst—wrote a column in which he said it's just indescribable. He said the Republican Party has become a group of crazed radicals dedicated to reactionary policies.[3]

It's not just their response to the pandemic. The Republicans have been holding the country hostage by refusing to agree to the perfectly normal procedure of raising the debt ceiling. When Trump was in office, he made a huge increase in the deficit with his lavish gifts to the rich. The Democrats went along and raised the debt ceiling every time it was necessary. Republicans won't do it unless conditions are imposed to block any form of vaccine mandate for small and medium-sized businesses. In other words, you want to harm the employees in a restaurant? Feel free to do it. It's your right to harm them. That's the Republican Party.

They also tried to cut off funding for Afghan refugees. I mean, the political leadership is just a gang of sadists. The shamelessness is indescribable. Take the hearing for Milley.

General Mark Milley, chairman of the Joint Chiefs of Staff.

He went through denunciations by a series of Republicans, Josh Hawley and a bunch of other frauds, condemning him for the withdrawal from Afghanistan. Take a look at the record. Until about a month ago, the Republican Party national website hailed the great genius Trump for arranging a much worse withdrawal. In February 2020, Trump simply gave away the store. He, of course, didn't inform the Afghan government, obviously not the Afghan people. Why should he care about them? He made an arrangement with the Taliban for US forces to withdraw in May 2021—the worst possible time, the beginning of the fighting season. Essentially no conditions. Do whatever you like. The only condition is, don't fire at US troops. It won't look good for me.

Biden came along, and somewhat improved the awful Trump arrangements. He put off the withdrawal a couple of months and added a few conditions that Trump hadn't put in place. The Republican Party was lauding Trump for his historic achievement until the moment when it began to collapse. Then they switched on a dime. All of them are berating Milley and others for carrying out an improved version of the policy that they had been lauding as a historic achievement when the hero that they worship was proposing it. The word *shameless* doesn't cover this. There's no words. It's a party that has totally gone rogue on issue after issue.

Large parts of Republicans are denying global warming. If you tune to Fox News and Breitbart, you're listening to the leadership of the Republican Party. That's all you hear. Maybe the virus is a bioweapon created by the Chinese to attack Americans. That's about a third of Republicans. Maybe Bill Gates is trying to put a chip in your head so he can control you. Maybe the government is run by an elite of sadistic pedophiles who are trying to torture children. That's about a quarter of Republicans. If you're stuck in that bubble, and that's what you're hearing from a political leadership that has lost even minimal commitment to the functioning of democracy, these are the results.

If you've lost any commitment to the country and to its people and to, of course, some form of democracy and you're solely committed to your own power and to the economic powers that you serve slavishly—concentrated wealth, the ultrawealthy, corporate power—if that's who you are, then this is a sensible way to behave. Of course, it will ruin the country, but who cares?

I can hear your critics saying, "It sounds like Chomsky is becoming an advocate for the Democratic Party." That's not the case.

Not in the least. Their policies are terrible. And most of what I write is criticism of the Democratic Party. I answered this question because you asked it. So, yes, if I'm asked what's going on, that's what's going on.

Take a look at the Democrats, and what I have actually been writing and speaking about. Let's start with August 9. The Intergovernmental Panel on Climate Change came out with its latest report—very dire.[4] It said, far more clearly than before, we're at a critical moment. We have to start reducing fossil fuels steadily right now, continuing until we're free of them by essentially mid-century. That's August 9. What happened on August 11? Joe Biden issued an appeal to OPEC, the oil cartel, to increase oil production so as to reduce gas prices in the United States, which will help his electoral prospects.[5] Is that the party we're supposed to be lauding?

There's plenty to condemn about the Democrats. They're a political party that does plenty of wrong things. They're not a rogue insurgency committed to serving a narrow constituency of extreme wealth and that doesn't give a damn how much they harm the country and the world. That's not a political party anymore. You can rank the Republicans among the ultraright parties in Europe with neofascist origins. They are off the spectrum.

The IPCC report—three thousand pages long, the work of more than two hundred scientists—warned of the dangers the planet is facing. Average global temperatures will likely rise 1.5 degrees Celsius, or 2.7 degrees Fahrenheit, by the year 2040. UN Secretary-General António Guterres called the report "a code red for humanity." He said, "If we combine forces now, we can avert climate catastrophe. But, as today's report makes clear, there is no time for delay and no room for excuses."[6]

There are mountains of evidence, which should be challenging the skeptics. Nevertheless, take our great neighbor to the north, Canada. Enbridge, a major Canadian corporation, is extending a pipeline from the tar sands in Alberta to Wisconsin. Tar sands being the dirtiest oil on the planet. And this is happening despite years of opposition from environmentalists and indigenous groups.

Canada's bad enough, and other countries aren't doing that wonderfully, but the United States is indescribable.

Take a look at the business press, especially the petroleum journals. The major oil companies are absolutely euphoric. They're beside themselves. They're finding new areas to explore. The US government continues to provide subsidies to fossil fuel companies. Republicans wouldn't tolerate anything else.

A former political organization now calling itself the Republican Party is dedicated to maximizing, accelerating the race to catastrophe. Take a look at the Republican states. Republican legislators aren't even trying to hide it. We have to race to catastrophe to enrich the energy corporations as much as possible before we reach apocalypse.

That's one part of the fading American democracy. Take a look at the one party that's still functioning, the Democratic Party. There's a major split within it, which offers the opportunity, at least, to push forward on the programs that can not only mitigate the crisis but also lead to a much better world. They are on the table.

There's a resolution by Representative Alexandria Ocasio-Cortez of New York and Senator Ed Markey of Massachusetts.[7] It gives a detailed outline of quite feasible proposals, well within cost range, that could, in fact, solve the crisis and lead the way to a much better society. It's a resolution. That's a step forward.

It reached this far because of extensive popular activism, mostly among young people, the Sunrise Movement and others, finally got to that point. The resolution, if you look at it, the details are approximately the same as what was produced by the International Energy Agency, originally a producer-based group, which recognized that we have to do something about climate change. Very similar to the quite detailed, extensive proposals of my coauthor, Robert Pollin, a leading economist who's worked hard on this, as has Jeffrey Sachs, another important economist whose somewhat different model comes out with pretty much the same conclusions.

It's all within range and can be done. It's on paper. Can you get it through? The Republicans are going to kill it. That's a given. They don't care what happens to the planet. They don't give a damn. They have other commitments to their own power and the superrich.

Take a look at the so-called negotiations that have been going on in Congress. The Republicans established an absolute red line: no increase in taxes for the superrich and the corporate sector. You cannot touch Trump's one legislative achievement, a tax scam that stabbed the country in the back, including the working classes and the middle classes, in order to enrich the very wealthy. That's a red line.

Furthermore, another red line is you can't fund the Internal Revenue Service to enable it to catch tax cheaters, rich people and corporations with huge numbers of corporate lawyers who figure out how to rob the population of trillions of dollars. You can't fund the IRS to investigate them.

That's the former Republican Party. We're looking at a group of radical sadists. Let's say it straight out. That's what it is.

Turn to the Democrats. They're split. The Clintonite-Obama type, neoliberal, Wall Street–oriented Democrats, who pretty much run the party apparatus, are reluctant. They're not going to push. And some of the right-wing Democrats mislabeled "moderate"—like Joe Manchin and Kyrsten Sinema, total cynics, flush with corporate money—are holding back on even minimal things. Sinema, for example, won't even say what she would agree to in the reconciliation bill. What would you agree to? Sorry, can't say.

The Democratic Party is split between these groups, on the one hand, and progressive, mostly young people, who are trying to save us from destruction on the climate, the pandemic, and the general breakdown of the society. The so-called reconciliation bill moves to give the population some respite from the neoliberal assault of the last forty years—some chance to respond to the major attack on the general population. There's nothing radical in it.

The United States has gone so far to the right that even policies that are normal in most of the rest of the world are considered radical. In fact, one of the editors of the *Financial Times*, in a semi-joke, said that if Bernie Sanders was in Germany, he could be running on the ticket of the Christian Democrats, which happens to be true.[8]

There was an article recently in the *New York Times* by Gregory Mankiw, a conservative Harvard economist, saying, well, yes, we don't have good social policies, but we make up for it by having a higher GDP per capita.[9] He failed to add one small point: workers in the United States work many more hours than workers in Europe. In Germany, workers get a month or more guaranteed vacation. Most of Europe has something similar. If people work 10 percent more, you're going to have a higher GDP. A big insight.

That's the kind of thing we're living with. You can't talk about the simplest things. We're living with a collapse of the social order after the major assault for the last forty years. You have some attempt to recover, but moving back toward the kind of country that, say, Dwight Eisenhower would have welcomed is considered too radical to push forward. The Democratic right wing won't accept it. Well, where do we go from there?

UN Secretary-General Guterres says, "We continue to destroy the things on which we depend for life on Earth. Ice caps and glaciers continue to melt, sea-level rise is accelerating, the ocean is dying and biodiversity is collapsing . . . . We really are out of time. We must act now to prevent further irreversible damage."[10] We keep hearing these calls, which invariably mention tipping points. How many tipping points is it going to take before we tip over and into the abyss?

We can't predict precisely, but we are moving toward irreversible tipping points. Every year we wait, every month we wait, the problem gets harder to deal with. If we had dealt with it ten years ago, it would be much less dire today. There would be much easier ways to deal with the crisis. If we had dealt with it thirty years ago, when it was perfectly clear where we were heading, then it would be far easier.

You recall that the first Bush administration refused even to join the Kyoto Protocol. We have to keep to our high priorities: enrich the very rich, maintain massive profits for the corporate sector. What happens to the country and the world is secondary. The Democrats don't have a great record. They pretty much went along. But at least within the Democratic Party, you're talking in a political universe in which discussion and pressure are possible. That's how the country is divided now.

We don't know exactly when the tipping points will come. But they'll come. In fact, it's possible we may have reached them already. If not, we'll reach them pretty soon. We get to an irreversible tipping point, a series of them. It doesn't mean that everybody dies tomorrow. The country will survive. Other countries will survive. But we're on a course toward total apocalypse.

All of this is known. We don't have to rehearse it. It's very well established. There's really no debate about it, at least among rational people. There are, more importantly, clear measures to deal with it. And, in fact, some positive steps.

Take, say, West Virginia, where Senator Manchin is working very hard to harm the people of his state as much as he can in service to his corporate masters. But the population of West Virginia is beginning to see the light. It's a coal state. The United Mine Workers recently proposed a transition from a coal-based economy for West Virginia—which has to disappear, otherwise we won't be around—to a renewable energy economy.[11] They have the capacity to do it. The transition proposal takes into account the needs of the working people who will be affected by loss of jobs in the short run. New kinds of jobs, training, and better jobs are all part of the transition plan.

Bob Pollin has been quite active in working with labor unions in West Virginia, Ohio, and California. And many of them are moving in this direction. So, it is possible. Activists can do some-thing. They must, in fact. It's the only hope.

The Republican Party, for the moment at least, is almost a lost cause. I say *almost* because, if you look closely, younger Re-publicans are not as insane and despicable as the leadership. They are more open to concern about these issues. They're not Susan Collins and Josh Hawley. So, you can have some hope there. And that should be pressed.

I think the general population, including Republicans, is reachable. They're stuck in a Fox News and Republican leader-ship bubble, but that doesn't mean they can't be moved. It'll take work, but they're human beings who care about their children, care about the environment, and they can be reached.

In fact, among them are many committed environmentalists. It's very interesting to read Arlie Hochschild's book about the Louisiana Bayou, *Strangers in Our Own Land*.[12] She was working for years in an area which is bright red, solid Republican, called cancer alley. People are dying of cancer from the pollution from the chemical plants. They know it. They don't like it.

Hochschild was working with people who are dedicated envi-ronmentalists, working hard to clean the place up, turn away from the polluting industries.

An ultraright representative there wants to destroy every-thing. A number of people vote for this far-right Republican who is at the extreme of trying to destroy the environment. When she looked into it, people gave rational answers. People who would say they're in favor of saving the environment. So, what are they to do? A guy in a suit from Washington comes down here and tells us, "You can't fish because the Bayou is polluted." That's what he tells us. Does he do anything about the polluting industries? No. So why should I listen to him? Is that an irrational answer? I don't think so.

Well, those are people that can be reached, too. It's not a lost cause, but it's going to take serious committed work with sympathy, understanding, dedication. We don't have to cover up what's going on among the major criminals—the leadership of the former Republican Party, for example. There are plenty in the Democratic Party. Don't cover that up. But there are possibilities to move forward.

In the twenty-fifth anniversary preface of his classic book *Orientalism*, Edward Said wrote,

> Every single empire in its official discourse has said that it is not like all the others, that its circumstances are special, that it has a mission to enlighten, civilize, bring order and democracy, and that it uses force only as a last resort. And, sadder still, there always is a chorus of willing intellectuals to say calming words about benign or altruistic empires, as if one shouldn't trust the evidence of one's eyes watching the destruction and the misery and death brought by the latest mission civilizatrice.[13]

Did the United States in Afghanistan and Iraq and elsewhere replicate what Said wrote?

He's absolutely right. It's exactly correct.

What's called American exceptionalism is mistaken in two respects. For one thing, the claims about what makes us exceptional are easily disproven. For another, there's nothing exceptional about it. It was the same with every other major power.

While France was officially committed to "exterminating" the Algerians, the slogan of the minister of war, French intellectuals were praising the civilizing mission of France.

While Britain was carrying out some of its worst atrocities in India—with huge massacres repressing an Indian uprising, moves to invade and conquer more of India, so that Britain could extend its monopoly of the opium trade—John Stuart Mill, a respectable intellectual, knew all about it. He was an official of the East India Company. Mill wrote an essay on intervention, which is read in law schools today as if it was an opposition to intervention.[14] But when you read it, it turns out what he was saying is, Britain is such an angelic power that others can't understand us. They heap obloquy upon us. They cannot perceive our dedication to the highest goals, and that includes bringing civilization to barbaric India. It's our responsibility to do it by smashing them in the face, murdering them, conquering them to extend our opium monopoly so we can break into China. He didn't say that part. I added it. But that's what he knew was happening. Well, that's John Stuart Mill, not a right-winger, at the peak of human enlightenment.

We can go on. If we had records from Attila the Hun, we'd probably find the same thing. You have to try hard to find an exception in human history. I can't find one.

Said is right. The role of the intellectuals is to praise it, to say how wonderful we are. Maybe we make mistakes. After all, anybody can make mistakes. But we're basically dedicated to the highest good.

I hate to repeat it, but I've been writing about this for fifty years.

In a book you wrote a decade ago with the Israeli historian Ilan Pappé, *Gaza in Crisis*, you have a chapter entitled, "'Exterminate All the Brutes': Gaza 2009," quoting the deranged Kurtz character in Joseph Conrad's novel *Heart of Darkness*.[15]

Actually, I was borrowing the word *exterminate* from a more directly relevant source, John Quincy Adams, the US secretary of state and president and the intellectual father of Manifest Destiny. He was responsible for some major atrocities, the Seminole War in Florida and others. In his later years, when he was reflecting on what happened, he lamented the fate of—I'm quoting him now—"that hapless race of native Americans, which we are exterminating with such merciless and perfidious cruelty."[16] That was before the worst of the atrocities, which were in California. That's the father of Manifest Destiny.

They knew what they were doing. The secretary of war under Washington, Henry Knox, said something similar. George Washington said that the Indians are like wolves, savages in human form, beasts that have to be driven into the wilderness. George Washington was known by the Iroquois as the "town destroyer" because, even before the Revolutionary War was over, he launched a major campaign of destruction among the Iroquois nations.

There were exceptions, of course, here and there, there always are. But that's the overwhelming pattern.

Let's now move to Afghanistan and the comparisons that the armchair pundits have been making to Saigon in 1975. In an interview I did with him in early September, Tariq Ali, who's not one of those armchair pundits, called what happened in Afghanistan "a huge blow to the American empire." And added, "No amount of spin can cover up the debacle."[17] Is it a bit early to be writing the obituary of the American empire?

I think as far as the American empire is concerned, it's a blip. Literally a blip.

From the point of view of the American empire, the invasion of Afghanistan was a mistake. George W. Bush and his surrounding courtiers Donald Rumsfeld and Dick Cheney decided to invade Afghanistan without any strategic objective. I think the best description of what they were doing was given by the most respected figure of the anti-Taliban resistance in Afghanistan, Abdul Haq. In fall 2001, he had an important interview with Anatol Lieven, who's a specialist on Central Asia.[18] Lieven asked him why he thought the United States was invading, and Haq said, "The US is trying to show its muscle, score a victory and scare everyone in the world." And he explained that the invasion was undermining efforts to overthrow the Taliban from within, which were feasible. But, he said, "they don't care about the suffering of the Afghans or how many people we will lose."

That's pretty much what Donald Rumsfeld was saying. At the time, the Taliban offered to surrender totally, which of course meant giving up any remnants of Al-Qaeda that were in Afghanistan. Rumsfeld's answer was, we do not "negotiate surrenders."[19] We want to smash you to pieces. He didn't say it in those words—I'm adding what was in his head. We want to smash you to pieces to show our muscle, intimidate everyone, then go on to our real targets. We don't care about Afghanistan. We want to go on to Iraq, major target, then on to the rest of the Middle East.

So, pulling out of Afghanistan is in fact, withdrawing from a mistake for once. Afghanistan didn't have the kind of strategic objectives that the Vietnam War did, which were, incidentally, partially achieved. Vietnam War was partially a success. If you look back at the original motivations, back in the early 1950s, they were largely achieved. In Afghanistan, nothing was achieved. It was a mistake. Of course, it's a disaster for Afghans, but that's not our concern.

Now, the question is, can we do something for compensation? Can we help them in some way? Well, what we ought to be doing is joining with the regional powers—China, Central Asian governments, Tajikistan, Uzbekistan, Pakistan, Russia—to offer whatever assistance we can to the Afghans to overcome the crisis of forty years of war, which we were involved in all along. They're desperate, they're starving, they don't have food. We can help.

What we're actually doing is holding on to their funds, which happen to be in the New York banks, and not giving them back. Pressuring the IMF and the World Bank not to give loans. We actually are joining with India—your favorite country[20]—to undermine the efforts of the Shanghai Cooperation Organization to assist the Afghans.

So that's what we can do now. As well as, of course, providing ample assistance to the Afghan refugees. That's our first responsibility. Unfortunately, we have a sadistic organization that controls half the government, which just today tried to cut aid to Afghans from the agreement to raise the debt ceiling.

Well, fortunately, that didn't work. That's the country we're in.

In your book *Climate Crisis and the Global Green New Deal*, you say, "I was involved in civil disobedience for many years, during some periods intensely, and think it's a reasonable tactic—sometimes."[21] Why sometimes?

Sometimes it's counterproductive.

In what way?

If it brings a backlash that is worse than the action itself, because people aren't prepared to understand it. To be an effective tactic, civil disobedience has to follow educational programs that bring the target audience to understand what you're doing. I have good friends I greatly respect who don't understand this. I think they're marvelous people. Quaker activists, Catholic activists who go into the submarine base in Connecticut and smash the hulls of nuclear submarines without any preparation for it. So, of course, the workforce is infuriated. Why are you taking our jobs? What the hell are you doing? A bunch of crazies. The general community doesn't understand what's going on.

They go to trial. They get to stand up and say, "God told me to do it," or whatever their rationale. A lot of movement resources are devoted to defending them at the trial. You go down and testify. What's the achievement? It's negative. Well, that's civil disobedience from really marvelous people who just aren't thinking that civil disobedience is a tactic. It's not a principle. It's a tactic undertaken to try to protect victims. That's when you undertake it. Otherwise, no.

You don't do crossword puzzles. But for years in the *New York Times*, your clue was "Linguist Chomsky." Well, on September 21, they changed the clue. Now it's "Author/activist Chomsky."

And the answer is four letters. With a recent crossword puzzle in the *Economist* and a *New York Times* in which your name is a clue, is there a danger you're going mainstream?[22]

I wouldn't worry about it.

What do you have coming up?

Constant interviews, articles, working on longer-term projects. There's another part of my brain that keeps functioning on scientific issues. There are lots of interesting new discoveries. I am hoping to write a technical monograph on them.

OPTIMISM OF THE WILL

Oro Valley, Arizona   December 9, 2021

What we are facing is often described as unprecedented. A pandemic, climate catastrophe, and always lurking off center stage, nuclear annihilation. Three of the four horsemen of the apocalypse.

I can add a fourth: the impending destruction of what remains of American democracy, and the shift of the United States toward a deeply authoritarian, also a protofascist, state, when the Republicans come back into office, which looks likely. So, that's four horses. And that has a big effect on the world and on the other three.

Remember that the Republicans are the denialist party. The party that is committed to racing to climate destruction with abandon, as quickly as possible in the hands of the chief wrecker, who they now worship like a demigod. It's bad news for the United States and for the world, given US power.

The International Institute for Democracy and Electoral Assistance just issued the *Global State of Democracy Report 2021*. It says that the United States is a country where democracy is "backsliding."[1]

Very severely. The Republican Party is openly dedicated—it's not even concealed—to undermining what remains of American

187

democracy. They're working very hard on it. There's quite an interesting article by Barton Gellman in the current *Atlantic*, which is worth reading carefully, that runs through a lot of the details.[2]

The Republicans have long understood, back to Nixon, that they're fundamentally a minority party. They're not going to be able to get votes by advertising their increasingly open commitment to the welfare of the ultrarich and the corporate sector. So, they've been diverting attention to other issues, as much as they can—so-called cultural issues.

It began with Nixon's Southern strategy. Nixon realized, as apparently LBJ had as well, that with limited Democratic support for civil rights legislation, they would lose Southern Democrats, who were openly and overtly extreme racists. The Nixon administration capitalized on that with their Southern strategy, hinting, not so subtly, that the Republicans would become the party of white supremacy.

In subsequent years, they picked up other issues. It's now the virtual definition of the party. So, let's run on attacking Critical Race Theory, whatever that means. A cover term, as their leading spokesmen have explained, for everything we can rally the public on: white supremacy, racism, misogyny, Christianity, abortion rights. Whatever we can pick up, we'll mobilize people on that.

Meanwhile, at the same time, the leadership, with the aid of the right-wing Federalist Society, has been developing legal means—if you want to call it that—for the Republicans to ensure that even as a minority party they will nevertheless be able to control the voting apparatus and the outcome of elections, exploiting the radically undemocratic features that are built into the constitutional system and the structural advantages that Republicans have as a party representing the more scattered, rural populations, the more traditionally Christian, white nationalist population. And using these advantages, even with a minority of the vote, they should be able to maintain something like almost permanent power.

Actually, the permanence won't be long if Trump or a Trump clone comes back into office in 2024. It's not very likely that the United States and, in fact, the world will be able to escape the impact of the climate destruction and environmental destruction that they are committed to accelerating.

We all saw what happened in Washington on January 6. Do you see the possibility of civil unrest spreading in the United States? There are multiple militias across the country. Representative Paul Gosar, of the great state of Arizona, and Representative Lauren Boebert, of the great state of Colorado, among others, have made threatening statements inciting violence and hatred. The internet is rife with conspiracy theories. What must we do?

It is very serious; in fact, maybe a third or so of Republicans think it may be necessary to use force to "save our country," as they put it. "Save our country" has a clear meaning. If anyone didn't understand it, Trump issued a call to people to mobilize to prevent the Democrats from swamping the country with criminals who are being let out of jails in other countries, so that the Democrats "replace" white Americans, and to carry out the destruction of America. The "great replacement." That's what "take away our country" means. And it's being used very effectively by proto-fascist elements, Trump being the most extreme and the most successful.

What can we do about it? The only tools available, like it or not, are education and organization. There's no other way. It means trying to revive a real authentic labor movement of the kind that has existed in the past and has been in the forefront of moves toward social justice; organizing other popular movements; carrying out widespread educational efforts to combat the brutal, murderous anti-vaccine campaigns that are going on. Make sure that there are serious efforts to deal with the climate crisis. Mobilize against the bipartisan commitment to increase dangerous military spending and to increase provocative actions against China, which could lead to a conflict that nobody wants, and could end up into a terminal war.

You just have to keep working on this. Nothing else. There are plenty of people doing this work—and their efforts have to be expanded through more support, more dedication. There is no other way.

But time is not on our side.

It doesn't matter. Whatever opportunities there are, we take them. They exist.

We can lament the fact that the stars are not aligned properly, but the only way to respond is by further dedicated engagement and careful thinking about how to structure actions and frame them.

In the background is the extreme inequality of the United States, which is just off the charts. Why is the United States so unequal?

It goes back a long way. A lot of this has happened in the last forty years, as part of the neoliberal assault on the general population, in which the Democrats have participated as well. Not to the extent of the Republicans, but the Democrats have also played their role.

There is a fairly careful estimate of what's called the transfer of wealth from the lower 90 percent of the population to the top 1 percent, actually, a fraction of them, during the four decades of this assault. A RAND Corporation study estimated it as close to $50 trillion.[3] That's a lot. It's not pennies. And it's ongoing.

During the pandemic, the measures that we're taking to save the economy from collapse did lead to further enrichment of the very few. They sort of maintained life for the others, but the Republicans are busy trying to dismantle that part. Leave only the part that enriches the very few. That's their dedication.

Take ALEC, the American Legislative Exchange Council. This goes back years. It's an organization funded by almost the entire corporate sector, which is dedicated to hitting at the weak point in the constitutional system, the states. It's very easy. It doesn't take much to buy or impel legislative representatives at the state level. So, what ALEC has been doing is working at the state level to impose legislation that will foster, for the long term, efforts of those who are seeking to destroy democracy, to increase radical inequality, to destroy the environment. Let's act at the state level to establish legislation that will foster and advance their efforts.

And one of the most important is to get the states to legislate that they cannot even investigate, and certainly not punish, wage theft.[4] Wage theft steals billions of dollars from workers every year by refusing to pay overtime and by other devices. There have been efforts to investigate it, but the business sector wants to stop them.

That's the state level. An analog of ensuring that the IRS not go after wealthy, corporate tax cheats.

At every level you can think of, this class war on the part of the masters, the corporate sector, the superrich is raging with intensity. And they're going to use every means they can to ensure that it goes on as long as possible, until they've succeeded in destroying, not only American democracy, but also the possibility of survival of organized society.

Corporate power seems unstoppable. The uber class of gazillionaires—Jeff Bezos, Richard Branson, and Elon Musk—are flying into outer space. But I'm reminded of something that the novelist Ursula K. Le Guin said some years ago: "We live in capitalism, its power seems inescapable." And then she adds, "So did the divine right of kings."[5]

So did slavery. So did the principle that women are property, which formerly lasted in the United States until the 1970s. So did laws against miscegenation, so extreme that the Nazis wouldn't accept them, which lasted in the United States until the 1960s.

All kinds of horrors have existed. Over time, their power has been eroded but never completely disappeared. Slavery was abolished, but its remnants remain in new and vicious forms. It's not slavery, but it's horrifying enough. The idea that women are not persons has been formally overcome, and overcome in practice, to a substantial extent. But there's plenty to do. The constitutional system was a step forward in the eighteenth century. Even the phrase "We the people" terrified the autocratic rulers of Europe, who were deeply concerned that the evils of democracy, what was then called republicanism, could spread and undermine civilized life. They were deeply concerned about that. Well, it did spread—and civilized life continued, even improved.

So, yes, there are periods of regression. There's progress. The class war never ends. The masters never relent. They are always looking for every opportunity. If they are the only participants in class struggle, we will have regression. But they don't have to be, any more than in the past, as in the eloquent quote from Le Guin.

In your *Masters of Mankind* book, you have an essay, "Can Civilization Survive Really Existing Capitalism?"[6] You write, "Really existing capitalist democracy—RECD for short (pronounced 'wrecked')" is "radically incompatible" with democracy and add that "it seems to me unlikely that civilization can survive really existing capitalism and the sharply attenuated democracy that goes along with it. Could functioning democracy make a difference? Consideration of nonexistent systems can only be speculative, but I think there's some reason to think so."[7] Tell me your reasons.

First of all, we live in this world, not in some world we would like to imagine. And in this world, if you simply think about the timescale for dealing with environmental destruction, it is far shorter than the time that would be necessary to carry out significant reshaping of basic institutions. That doesn't mean you have to abandon the attempt to do that. You should be doing that, all the time. You should be working on ways to raise consciousness, raise understanding, build the rudiments of future institutions in the present society.

At the same time, the measures to save us from self-destruction will have to take place within the basic framework of existing institutions. Some modification of them, but without fundamental change. And it can be done. We know how it can be done.

Meanwhile, work should continue on overcoming the problem of RECD, really existing capitalist democracy, which in its basic nature is a death sentence and also deeply inhuman in its fundamental properties. So, let's work on that, and at the same time, ensure that we save the possibility of achieving it by overcoming the immediate and urgent crisis.

You and I and others are often accused of just talking about gloom and doom. But here are a couple of developments that are quite positive. The first one being, What happened in India, where thousands of Indian farmers from Punjab and neighboring states encamped outside of Delhi, and, after a yearlong struggle, forced the Hindu nationalist regime to roll back three agricultural laws that would have reduced farmers to a semi-serf status.

The other positive piece of news is the election of Xiomara Castro as president of Honduras, the first woman to hold that post. She replaces a corrupt right-wing regime that had ruled for twelve years. She's described as a democratic socialist. She's the wife of Manuel Zelaya, who was president but was overthrown in a coup in 2009. Talk about those two examples.

I could add a third one. Lula just announced his presidency campaign for Brazil, and he's running way above Bolsonaro in the polls. That could lead to a reversal of the move toward protofascism in the second-largest country in the hemisphere.

These two things that you mention are major victories. The farmers' strike in India was an astonishing development. These are farmers who have suffered severely through the neoliberal period. The support systems for rural agriculture have been undermined—rural development programs, research programs. The system has been redesigned so that farming life is so painful and difficult that suicides have been rising sharply. The numbers are appalling. This has been going on for years, ever since the neoliberal rules were imposed.

The farmers finally rose up against the latest effort of the Modi government in huge numbers, a massive strike. They withstood the violence and repression and couldn't be beaten down. They stayed there, persistent, over a year, and finally won. The government backed down. It's a very right-wing government and has a lot of voting support, but it had to back down. That's of extreme importance. It's deeply encouraging. It shows what the people can do when they refuse to be servants of the masters.

Honduras has a hideous history. Way back, it was the prototypical so-called banana republic, run by a dozen or so rich families, with awful conditions for most of the population. During the 1980s, it was the US military base for Reagan's terrorist wars in Central America. There was plenty of repression in Honduras as well. Finally, a moderately reformist candidate, Manuel Zelaya, appeared. Zelaya was from the conservative movement, but he had some moderately reformist efforts.

The ruling class came down on Zelaya like a ton of bricks. He was forced out of office, expelled from the country. The military coup was harshly condemned by almost all of Latin America and most of the world, with the exception of Obama and Hillary Clinton, who gave it a light tap on the wrist but refused to call it a military coup, which it obviously was, because if they'd called it a military coup, they would have had to withdraw US military support for the ruling junta, which was destroying Honduran democracy. And they didn't want to do that.

So, it wasn't a coup. And that led to a sharp increase in the Honduran horror story. It became basically the murder capital of the world. People began to flee in desperation. It was the source of the caravans that the US government tried to get other countries to block so they wouldn't reach our border. They have been the plurality of people fleeing from Central America.

The ruling junta did then carry out an election, which was ridiculed virtually everywhere, except in Washington, where Obama and Clinton praised the military junta for their promising steps toward democracy. Then, apart from all the other crimes, Honduras turned into one of the major narcotrafficking centers. The Colombian cartels were using Honduras to ship drugs to the Mexican cartels and then into the United States. The president's brother was deeply implicated in this, and the president himself was surely involved.

The president was Juan Orlando Hernández.

Yes, that's Honduras under our rule, for a century. Now, as you say, the population did manage to elect Xiomara Castro, who might be able to carry out the mild reforms that her husband was beginning to initiate. There will be plenty of roadblocks from the same internal forces that overthrew Zelaya and drove him into exile—and the same US forces that have backed them. It's up to us to ensure that that's not overturned. But it could be. There's going to be a battle.

Similar battles are taking place elsewhere: Peru, Colombia, Brazil, Haiti, all the areas that are our so-called backyard. In all these countries, we have an overwhelming influence, it has been used overwhelmingly for harm and destruction. It doesn't have to be. That's our choice, here. We can change that.

I would add Chile to that list of countries you just named. Now, when the president says, "America is back," what does that mean?[8]

Biden was addressing Europe. The only thing Trump understood was how to serve the rich and how to wreck. Those were his policies. So, one of the things he wrecked was European alliances, and Biden was saying, don't worry. We're going to rejoin you in the alliances of the past, which don't have a very lovely record, I should say.

Biden's saying we are going to rejoin the Paris climate agreement that Trump pulled out of. He claimed that they would make some moves to renew the Iran nuclear deal that Trump had destroyed. A few other measures. But basically, US policy didn't change very much. Some of the more gratuitously sadistic elements of Trump's policies that had no geopolitical significance were reversed, but the fundamental policies remain, and in some ways are becoming even harsher.

So, take, say, Ukraine. The far-right Fox News commentator Tucker Carlson made the comment that should be the leading element of policy. Whatever you think about Putin, maybe the rottenest person in the world, he's not trying to conquer Europe. He's not even trying to conquer Ukraine. He's trying to protect Russian borders from what is, from the Russian point of view, a very serious threat.[9] That's Tucker Carlson, and he's correct.

Meanwhile, the Biden administration is sending hawks like Victoria Nuland to try to increase the tensions. I'm not saying they're trying to do this, but that's the consequence—to raise the possibility of a confrontation that can be settled by diplomacy and negotiations. They are raising tensions with Russia, as in the case of China, to a level that might lead to a very serious conflict, even terminal war.

We have to turn to Tucker Carlson for sanity on the topic. I don't know what his motives are. Whatever they are, the comment was the right one. And the fact that it's coming from the extreme right is a terrible condemnation of our political system. It should be coming from the sane, liberal center, and obviously from the left.

Much of the mainstream media, not just Tucker Carlson, is awash in reports about what is called the China threat. Recently, you were on Pakistan's Daanish TV, and you said China "is not subordinate to the United States. It cannot be intimidated by the United States. It's not like Europe, and that's unacceptable. If you're the global dominant hegemon, the mafia don, basically you can't accept successful defiance."[10] China's not like Europe, you say. Can Europe be pushed around? Is that what you mean?

You see it every moment. Take the phrase "successful defiance." That comes from the State Department Policy Planning Council in 1964. They were talking about Cuba and the Cuban threat. The threat of Cuba is Cuba's "successful defiance" of US policies going back one hundred and fifty years.[11] That means to the 1820s, going back to the Monroe Doctrine, which announced Washington's intention to dominate the hemisphere.

The Monroe Doctrine was just words at the time. Britain was far too powerful for the United States to dominate the hemisphere. But that was the goal. And Cuba, today and since the 1960s, is successfully defying our goal, which of course by that time the United States eventually succeeded in achieving.

The founders anticipated that Britain would decline, and the United States would increase in power sooner or later. As John Quincy Adams put it, Cuba would fall into our hands by the laws of political "gravitation" the way an apple falls from the tree, and we would extend our domination over the hemisphere.[12] Well, that happened. Cuba was beginning to defy this by 1960. And successful defiance cannot be tolerated. The US launched major terrorist wars, which we don't talk about here, but they were very serious. They almost led to a terminal nuclear war. A severe blockade. It's a small island country that's in the shadow of the United States. It can barely survive this. It's amazing that they have survived.

Now, let's go to Europe and being pushed around. Europe strongly opposes this, as the entire world does. We see that every year, at the United Nations, when the General Assembly has a vote on the US embargo, sanctions, and blockade of Cuba. This last year, it was nearly unanimous. One hundred eighty-four to two, with three abstentions, against the United States.[13] The two against are the United States and Israel, a client state that votes reflexively with the master. All of Europe strongly opposes the embargo, but they abide by it. Same with Iran.

Of course, they have reasons. If you defy the master, the godfather, you get punished. The US has weapons. One of them is straightforward. You're thrown out of the international financial system, which is run from New York. Well, not a small thing. Afghanistan, right now, a million Afghans are facing starvation while the United States withholds the funds from the government that happen to be sequestered in New York banks and, according to the press reports, has been pressuring the international institutions to withhold support from them while Afghans die of starvation. I hate to use the appropriate word, but that's a small-scale example of the fact that you can't tolerate successful defiance. There are many others.

Take the island of Grenada, the nutmeg capital of the world, a very powerful force—you can't find it on a map. They had a reformist leader, Maurice Bishop, in the 1970s who began to carry out very mild reforms: starting a fishing cooperative, a couple more things. The Carter administration came down on them, quickly, launching efforts to isolate them and stop this defiance of US power.

In 1983, Reagan invaded, with a grand show of courage and manliness. Stood up proudly announcing that the United States stands up strong. Six thousand US forces were able to overcome the resistance of forty Cuban construction workers who had already agreed to allow the Americans to enter, but the Reagan administration pretended that it hadn't heard that so it could send in a show of force. Six thousand troops got eight thousand medals for their great courage. And Reagan projected himself as a major hero, strutting around to show that America's great again.

This was probably undertaken to drive off the front pages the fact that an attack in Lebanon at a US base had killed a couple hundred Marines. And that didn't look good. So, let's invade Grenada, and show how powerful and manly we are. Well, that's Grenada. No successful defiance.

But when it comes to China, you can't do it. They are not intimidated. They continue their programs. When I discussed the China threat, I was actually paraphrasing former prime minister of

Australia Paul Keating, a highly regarded international statesman. He published an article in which he analyzed the China threat.[14] He debunked every part of it, which is not very difficult, and ended up by concluding the China threat is that China exists. It exists. It's not intimidated. It's even doing really dangerous things. For example, recently it established plans for creating, I think, one thousand vocational schools in Southeast Asia, Africa, where students will be taught Chinese technology, which means that their countries will then be using advanced Chinese technology.

The United States is working very hard to prevent China's technological development and to prevent countries from using Chinese technology. China's going around us, setting up vocational schools where students will be trained in advanced technology, improving their own countries, and indebted to China for doing it. How can a country sink to that level of barbarism? We really have to work hard to prevent it. And the only answers we seem to have are bombs. Somehow that doesn't seem like an effective weapon. So, there's a real China threat.

Plenty of things that China is doing are quite wrong, even abominable and merit severe condemnation. Some are even in violation of international law, but none of them are a threat. The US tolerates much worse behavior elsewhere. The China threat is exactly what Paul Keating said. Its existence is a rock that you can't move, and it is going to continue with its policies. It's expanding its programs through Central Asia, incorporating the region within a China-dominated system. The Shanghai Cooperation Organization, based in China, includes Russia, which has rich resources and a strong military system. It includes India and Pakistan. Iran is now a member, along with all the Central Asian states. It's very likely going to include Afghanistan pretty soon. China may begin to exploit Afghanistan's rich mineral resources, trying to shift its economy from opium production, which is what it's been under US rule, to mineral export. Maybe they'll succeed in this, maybe not.

China's eye is plainly on Turkey. Turkey is going bankrupt. China will presumably move to expand its already substantial influence in Turkey and into Eastern and Central Europe. It has development programs in Africa and is even encroaching in South America, US domains. The United States has been unable to do anything to stop it. It's tried, but all we're doing is increasing provocations in the seas around China, where China is doing things that are totally improper but that can be dealt with by diplomacy and negotiations, much as in the Ukraine case. But that's not going to be pursued under the hawkish national security advisers of the Biden administration. That's another thing that has to be changed, and fast.

Talk about the importance of independent progressive media such as *Democracy Now!* and Fairness & Accuracy in Reporting. And may I say, *Alternative Radio*? Publishers like Verso, Haymarket, Monthly Review, City Lights, and The New Press. Magazines like *Jacobin*, *The Nation*, *The Progressive*, and *In These Times*. Online magazines like TomDispatch, The Intercept, and ScheerPost. Community radio stations such as KGNU, WMNF, KPFK, and others. How important are they in countering the dominant corporate narrative?

What else is going to counter it? They are the ones who are holding up the hope that we'll be able to find ways to counter these highly harmful, destructive developments that we're discussing.

As I mentioned before, the core method, which we both know, is education. People have to come to understand what's happening in the world. That requires means to disseminate information and analysis, opening up opportunities for discussion, which you're not going to find, for the most part, in the mainstream. Maybe occasionally at the margins. But you'll rarely find them in the mainstream. A lot of what we've been talking about is not discussed at all, or only marginally, within the major media. So, these conversations have to be brought to the public through these other channels. There is no other way.

Actually, there is another way: organization. It is possible, and in fact easy, to conduct educational and cultural programs inside organizations. That was one of the major contributions of the labor movement when it was a vibrant, lively institution. One of the main reasons why Reagan and Thatcher were so determined to destroy labor, as they both did. Their first moves were attacks on the labor movement.

There were educational and cultural programs that brought people together to think about the world, to understand it, and develop ideas. It takes organization to do that. To do that alone as an isolated person is extremely difficult, if possible at all.

So, organization is a powerful means, along with independent media integrating with organizational efforts. Despite the corporate effort to beat back the unions, there was a lively, independent labor press in the United States as late as the 1950s, reaching lots of people, condemning what they called the "bought priesthood" of the mainstream press. It took a long time to destroy that. That can be revived.

There's a long history in the United States of a vibrant, progressive labor press, back to the nineteenth century, when it was a major phenomenon. That can be and should be revived as part of the revival of a militant, functioning labor movement at the forefront of progress toward social justice. It happened before and can happen again. And independent media are critical elements of this.

When I was a kid, in the 1930s and early 1940s, I could read Izzy Stone in the *Philadelphia Record*. It wasn't the major journal in Philadelphia. It was a small journal on the side, but it was there. Later, in the late 1940s, I could read him in *PM*, which was an independent journal. It made a huge difference. Not just Izzy Stone, but others like him.

Later in the 1950s and 1960s, the only way to read Stone was to subscribe to his newsletter. That was the independent media in the 1950s. In the 1960s, it began to pick up a little bit with

Ramparts, radio programs like Danny Schechter's on WBCN in Boston, and others like it here and there.

This continues around the country. The ones you mentioned are forces for independence, for thinking. It made a huge difference for me when I was growing up, to hear these things, to read them. And the same is true for others today.

There are multiple mentions of Antonio Gramsci in two of your most recent books, *Consequences of Capitalism* and *Climate Crisis and the Global Green New Deal*. Specifically his quote, "The crisis consists precisely in the fact that the old is dying and the new cannot be born; in this interregnum a great variety of morbid symptoms appear." Now, we've talked about that one. The other one, that I'd like you to address, is "Pessimism of the intellect, optimism of the will." Talk about Gramsci and his relevance today and the meaning of that quote.

Gramsci was a leading left labor activist in Italy around the late teens, early 1920s. He was very active in organizing left worker collectives, self-directed, kind of the left wing of the international communist, Marxist system.

In Italy, the fascist government took over in the early 1920s. One of their first acts was to send Gramsci to prison. The reasons were given by the prosecutor. The prosecutor stated, during the trial, we have to silence this voice. This gets back to the importance of independent media. We have to silence this voice. So, he was sent to prison.

Well, he wrote *Prison Notebooks*.[15] He wasn't silenced, though the public couldn't read him. He continued the work that he began and his writing, including some of the things you quoted. In the early 1930s, he wrote that the old world is collapsing, the new world has not yet risen. We are facing morbid symptoms. Mussolini was one, Hitler was another. Nazi Germany almost conquered large parts of the world. We came very close to that. The Russians defeated Hitler. Otherwise, half the world would probably be run by Nazi Germany. But it was very close. Morbid symptoms were visible everywhere.

The adage you quoted, "Pessimism of the intellect, optimism of the will," which became famous, came from the period when he was still able to publish. We must look at the world reasonably, without illusions, understand it, decide how to act, and recognize that there are grim portents. There are very dangerous things happening. That's pessimism of the intellect. At the same time, we recognize there are ways out. There are opportunities. There are the kinds of achievements that you mentioned—and many more ways of dealing with the crises we face. So, we have optimism of the will, meaning, we dedicate ourselves to using all the opportunities that are available, and they do exist, and working to overcome the morbid symptoms and move toward a more just and decent world.

In these dark times, it's difficult for many to feel there's a bright future ahead. You're always asked, what gives you hope? And I have to ask you the same question that so many others do.

One thing that gives hope is that people are struggling hard under very severe circumstances, much more severe than we can imagine, to achieve rights and justice. They don't give up hope. Like the farmers in India. Or the people living in misery in Honduras. They don't give up, so we certainly can't.

The other is that there's simply no option. The alternative to giving up hope is to say, okay, I'll help the worst to happen. That's the choice. You can say, I'll refuse to engage in the opportunities that are available—I'll help ensure that the worst will happen as quickly as possible. That's one choice. The other is, I'll try to do as best I can, what the farmers in India are doing, what poor and miserable peasants in Honduras are doing, and many others like them throughout the world. I'll do that as best I can. And maybe we can get to a decent world in which people can feel that they can live without shame. A better world.

So, that's not much of a choice. We can easily make it.

NOTES

1. The Decision that Has to Be Made

1. Carol Morello, "US Warns Allies to Cut Imports of Iranian Oil," *Washington Post*, June 27, 2018.

2. John R. Bolton, "To Stop Iran's Bomb, Bomb Iran," *New York Times*, March 26, 2015.

3. Natalie Andrews and Dion Nissenbaum, "Senate Passes Resolution to Withdraw U.S. Support for War in Yemen," *Wall Street Journal*, December 13, 2018.

4. Arthur M. Schlesinger Jr., "Report to the President on Latin American Mission: February 12–March 3, 1961," *Foreign Relations of the United States, 1961–1963*, vol. 12, *American Republics*, Record No. 7 (Washington: U.S. Government Printing Office, 1996), 13.

5. Policy Planning Staff, "Review of Current Trends; U.S. Foreign Policy," February 24, 1948, in *Foreign Relations of the United States, 1948*, vol. 1, part 2 ("General, The United Nations"), (Washington: U.S. Government Printing Office, 1976), 511.

6. Walter LaFeber, *Inevitable Revolutions: The United States in Central America* (New York: W. W. Norton, 1983), 109.

7. Sean Kenji Starrs, *American Power Globalized: Rethinking National Power in the Age of Globalization* (New York: Oxford University Press, forthcoming). See also Sean Kenji Starrs, "American Economic Power Hasn't Declined—It Globalized! Summoning the Data and Taking Globalization Seriously," *International Studies Quarterly* 57, no. 4 (2013): 817–30.

8.   Noam Chomsky and David Barsamian, *Global Discontents: Conversations on the Rising Threats to Democracy* (New York: Metropolitan Books, 2017), 187.

9.   United Nations Security Council, Resolution 687, April 3, 1991.

10. Lee Fang, "Arms Manufacturers Tell Investors that Iran Tension Fuels Business," The Intercept, May 28, 2019, https://theintercept .com/2019/05/28/arms-manufacturers-investors-iran-business/.

11. William Hartung, "Recent Pentagon Increases Exceed Russia's Entire Military Budget," Institute for Public Accuracy, June 26, 2018, https://accuracy.org/release/recent-pentagon-increases -exceed-russias-entire-military-budget-interviews-available/.

12. Anne Case and Angus Deaton, *Deaths of Despair and the Future of Capitalism* (Princeton, NJ: Princeton University Press, 2020).

13. Ben Steverman, "The Wealth Detective Who Finds the Hidden Money of the Super Rich," *Bloomberg Businessweek*, May 23, 2019, https://www.bloomberg.com/news/features/2019-05-23/the-wealth -detective-who-finds-the-hidden-money-of-the-super-rich.

14. Pamela Haag, *The Gunning of America: Business and the Making of American Gun Culture* (New York: Basic Books, 2016).

15. Thorstein Veblen, *The Theory of the Leisure Class* (New York: Oxford University Press, 2009).

16. *District of Columbia v. Heller*, 554 U.S. 570 (2008).

17. Court of King's Bench, *Somerset v. Stewart*, 98 ER 499 (1772).

18. Daniela Diaz, "Trump: I'm a 'Very Stable Genius,'" CNN, January 6, 2018; Brett Samuels, "Trump Ramps Up Rhetoric on Media, Calls Press 'The Enemy of the People," The Hill, April 5, 2019.

19. Robert Weissman, "Trump's Emergency Declaration Is Abuse of Power," Public Citizen, February 15, 2019, https://www.citizen.org /news/trumps-emergency-declaration-is-abuse-of-power-public -citizen-will-challenge-it-urge-congress-to-overturn-quickly/.

20. Thomas E. Mann and Norman Jay Ornstein, "Finding the Common Good in an Era of Dysfunctional Governance," *Daedalus*, Spring 2013, https://www.amacad.org/publication /finding-common-good-era-dysfunctional-governance.

21. Carl Hulse, "McConnell Vows to Vote on Supreme Court Nominee Four Years after Blocking One," *New York Times*,

September 18, 2020, https://www.nytimes.com/2020/09/18/us
/elections/mcconnell-vows-to-vote-on-supreme-court-nominee
-four-years-after-blocking-one.html.

22. Patricia Cohen, "Planting the Seeds of a Story With Farmers in
the Midwest," *New York Times*, May 31, 2019, https://www
.nytimes.com/2019/05/31/reader-center/planting-corn
-interviewing-soybean-farmers.html.

23. Taylor Telford, "Here's How Tariffs Will Raise Prices at Some
of America's Best-Known Companies," *Washington Post*, June 7,
2019.

24. Maureen Dowd, "Crazy Is as Crazy Does," *New York Times*, May
25, 2019, https://www.nytimes.com/2019/05/25/opinion/sunday
/donald-trump-nancy-pelosi.html.

25. Juliet Eilperin, Brady Dennis, and Chris Mooney, "White House
Projects Earth Will Warm—And Accepts It," *Washington Post*,
September 30, 2018; Coral Davenport, "Trump Administration
Unveils Its Plan to Relax Car Pollution Rules," *New York Times*,
August 2, 2018, https://www.nytimes.com/2018/08/02/climate
/trump-auto-emissions-california.html?module=inline.

26. See Noam Chomsky and Robert Pollin, with C. J. Polychroniou,
Climate Crisis and the Global Green New Deal (New York: Verso
Books, 2020).

2. Threats to Peace and the Planet

1. "Something in the Air: Why Are So Many Countries
Witnessing Mass Protests?" *Economist*, November 4, 2019,
https://www.economist.com/international/2019/11/04/why-are
-so-many-countries-witnessing-mass-protests.

2. Stacy Torres, "The Protests in Chile Aren't about 30 Pesos. They're
about 30 Years of Failure," *Washington Post*, October 23, 2019.

3. See, among other studies, Steven H. Woolf et al., "Warning
Signs: Changes in Midlife Death Rates Across Racial and
Ethnic Groups in the United States," *BMJ*, June 25, 2018.

4. "What Brazil's President, Jair Bolsonaro, has said about Brazil's
Indigenous Peoples," Survival International, n.d., https://www
.survivalinternational.org/articles/3540-Bolsonaro.

5.   Dom Phillips, "Brazil: Tortured Dissidents Appalled by Bolsonaro's
     Praise for Dictatorship," *Guardian*, March 30, 2019, https://www
     .theguardian.com/world/2019/mar/30/brazil-bolsonaro-regime
     -military-dictatorship.

6.   "Bolsonaro Defende Guerra Civil No Brasil e Sonegação de
     Impostos em Vídeo de 1999," *Estado de Minas*, August 29, 2018,
     https://www.em.com.br/app/noticia/politica/2018/08/29/interna
     _politica,984474/bolsonaro-defende-guerra-civil-no-brasil-e
     -sonegacao-de-impostos-em-vi.shtml; Chico Marés,
     "#Verificamos: É Verdade que Bolsonaro Elogiou Vavalaria Norte-
     Americana por Dizimar Indios," *Folha de S.Paulo*, December 6,
     2018, https://piaui.folha.uol.com.br/lupa/2018/12/06
     /verificamos-bolsonaro-cavalaria/.

7.   Ruth Leacock, *Requiem for Revolution: The United States and
     Brazil, 1961–1969* (Kent, OH: Kent State University Press,
     1990), 197.

8.   Paul Ingram, Dan Shearer, and Jorge Encinas, "Bannon Boosts
     'Private' Border Wall at Sahuarita Event," *Tucson Sentinel*,
     February 9, 2019, http://www.tucsonsentinel.com/local/report
     /020819_bannon_wall/bannon-boosts-private-border-wall
     -sahuarita-event/.

9.   Todd S. Purdum, with David Stout, "Bush Officials Say the Time
     Has Come for Action on Iraq," *New York Times*, September 9, 2002,
     https://www.nytimes.com/2002/09/09/international/middleeast
     /bush-officials-say-the-time-has-come-for-action-on.html.

10. Thomas Ferguson, Paul Jorgensen, and Jie Chen, "How Much
     Can the US Congress Resist Political Money? A Quantitative
     Assessment," Institute for New Economic Thinking, Working
     Paper Series No. 109, May 15, 2020, https://doi.org/10.36687
     /inetwp109.

11. Benjamin Carter Hett, *The Death of Democracy: Hitler's Rise to
     Power and the Downfall of the Weimar Republic* (New York: St.
     Martin's, 2019), 180.

12. Noam Chomsky, "We Must Stop War with Iran Before It's Too
     Late," *In These Times*, May 21, 2019, https://inthesetimes.com

/article/iran-war-trump-bolton-neoliberalism-venezuela-cuba
-world-order.

13. Paul Bond, "Leslie Moonves on Donald Trump: 'It May Not Be Good for America, but It's Damn Good for CBS,'" *Hollywood Reporter*, February 29, 2016, https://www.hollywoodreporter.com/news/general-news/leslie-moonves-donald-trump-may-871464/.

14. William J. Perry, "The Terrifying Lessons of Hawaii's Botched Missile Alert," Politico, January 15, 2018, https://www.politico.com/magazine/story/2018/01/15/the-terrifying-lessons-of-hawaiis-botched-missile-alert-216325/; See also William J. Perry, "One Man Shouldn't Control the Nuclear Button," *Wall Street Journal*, October 4, 2021, https://www.wsj.com/articles/nuclear-button-launch-general-milley-unauthorized-trump-china-11633359093.

15. James Hansen, testimony before the United States Senate Committee on Energy and Natural Resources, June 23, 1988.

16. Katharine Hayhoe, "I'm a Climate Scientist Who Believes in God. Hear Me Out," *New York Times*, October 31, 2019, https://www.nytimes.com/2019/10/31/opinion/sunday/climate-change-evangelical-christian.html.

17. See Raymond Zhong, "Trends in Arctic Report Card: 'Consistent, Alarming and Undeniable,'" *New York Times*, December 14, 2021, https://www.nytimes.com/2021/12/14/climate/arctic-report-card-climate-change.html.

18. See Patrick Cockburn, *War in the Age of Trump: The Defeat of Isis, the Fall of the Kurds, the Conflict with Iran* (New York: Verso, 2020).

19. Gabriel Kolko, *Main Currents in Modern American History* (New York: Harper & Row, 1976).

20. United Nations News, "Gaza Could Become Uninhabitable in Less than Five Years Due to Ongoing 'De-development'—UN report," September 1, 2015, https://news.un.org/en/story/2015/09/507762-gaza-could-become-uninhabitable-less-five-years-due-ongoing-de-development-un.

3. The Politics of the Pandemic

1. Noam Chomsky, *Failed States: The Abuse of Power and the Assault on Democracy* (New York: Metropolitan Books, 2006), 2.
2. Bruce Livesey, "Have Americans Gone Crazy?" *National Observer*, May 5, 2020, https://www.nationalobserver.com/2020/05/05/opinion/have-americans-gone-crazy.
3. George Packer, "We Are Living in a Failed State," *Atlantic*, June 2020, https://www.theatlantic.com/magazine/archive/2020/06/underlying-conditions/610261/.
4. Jonathan Chait, "Top Government Vaccine Expert Fired for Questioning Trump's Fake Science," *New York Magazine*, April 22, 2020, https://nymag.com/intelligencer/2020/04/top-vaccine-expert-fired-trump-hydroxychloroquine-messonnier-science.html.
5. Peter Beinert, "Trump's Break with China Has Deadly Consequences," *Atlantic*, March 28, 2020, https://www.theatlantic.com/ideas/archive/2020/03breaking-china-exactly-wrong-answer/608911/.
6. Michael D. Shear, "Trump Attacks WHO over Criticisms of US Approach to Coronavirus," *New York Times*, April 7, 2020, https://www.nytimes.com/2020/04/07/us/politics/coronavirus-trump-who.html.
7. See "What's in President Trump's Fiscal 2021 Budget?" *New York Times*, February 10, 2020, https://www.nytimes.com/2020/02/10/business/economy/trump-budget-explained-facts.html; Alan Rappeport and Lola Fadulu, "Trump Budget Would Fray Social Safety Net," *New York Times*, February 10, 2020, https://www.nytimes.com/2020/02/10/us/trump-budget-safety-net-cuts.html; David E. Sanger, "Trump Budget Calls for New Nuclear Warheads and 2 Types of Missiles," *New York Times*, February 10, 2020, https://www.nytimes.com/2020/02/10/us/politics/trump-budget-nuclear-missiles.html; Margot Sanger-Katz, "In Trump's Budget, Big Health Care Cuts but Few Details," *New York Times*, February 10, 2020, https://www.nytimes.com/2020/02/10/upshot/health-care-trump-budget.html.
8. Ariel Dorfman, "I Warned of Trump's Attack on Science. But I Never Predicted the Horror that Lay Ahead," *Guardian*, April

12, 2020, https://www.theguardian.com/commentisfree/2020
/apr/12/i-warned-of-trumps-attack-on-science-but-i-never
-predicted-the-horror-that-lay-ahead.

9. Tom Phillips, "'So What?': Bolsonaro Shrugs Off Brazil's Rising
Coronavirus Death Toll," *Guardian*, April 29, 2020, https://www
.theguardian.com/world/2020/apr/29/so-what-bolsonaro-shrugs
-off-brazil-rising-coronavirus-death-toll.

10. Claudine Gartenberg and George Serafeim, "181 Top CEOs
Have Realized Companies Need a Purpose Beyond Profit,"
Harvard Business Review, August 20, 2019, https://hbr.org
/2019/08/181-top-ceos-have-realized-companies-need-a
-purpose-beyond-profit.

11. Jemima Kelly, "That Imperial Coronavirus Report, in Detail,"
Financial Times, March 17, 2020, https://www.ft.com/content
/1fed7551-61ce-41de-bad3-a38534b0ada8; David Spiegelhalter
and Anthony Masters, "How Good Are We at Predicting the
Pandemic?" *Guardian*, May 9, 2020, https://www
.theguardian.com/theobserver/commentisfree/2021/may/09
/how-good-are-we-at-predicting-pandemic.

12. Jason Slotkin, "Birx On 'Stay-At-Home' Protests: 'Devastatingly
Worrisome,'" National Public Radio, May 3, 2020, https://www
.npr.org/sections/coronavirus-live-updates/2020/05/03/849786763
/birx-on-stay-at-home-protests-devastatingly-worrisome.

13. Stephen Bezruchka, "The Coronavirus Pandemic," Seattle, WA,
March 14, 2020. Talk available from *Alternative Radio* at https://
www.alternativeradio.org/products/bezs011/.

14. Brooke Jarvis, "The Insect Apocalypse Is Here," *New York Times*,
November 27, 2018, https://www.nytimes.com/2018/11/27
/magazine/insect-apocalypse.html.

15. Paul Krugman, "Republicans Are Still Waging War on
Workers," *New York Times*, May 10, 2021, https://www.nytimes
.com/2021/05/10/opinion/jobs-unemployment-benefits
-republicans.html.

16. Natalie Kitroeff, "As Workers Fall Ill, US Presses Mexico to Keep
American-Owned Plants Open," *New York Times*, April 30, 2020,

https://www.nytimes.com/2020/04/30/world/americas
/coronavirus-mexico-factories.html.

17. Juan González, "Make No Mistake: This Country Is Edging
    Closer to Neo-Fascist Authoritarianism," *Democracy Now!*, April
    21, 2020, https://www.democracynow.org/2020/4/21
    /juan_gonzalez_coronavirus_update.

18. Rob Larson, *Bit Tyrants: The Political Economy of Silicon Valley*
    (Chicago: Haymarket Books, 2020).

19. Shoshana Zuboff, *The Age of Surveillance Capitalism: The Fight
    for a Human Future at the New Frontier of Power* (New York:
    PublicAffairs, 2019).

4. The President, the Pandemic, and the Election

1. Editors, "Dying in a Leadership Vacuum," *New England Journal
    of Medicine*, October 8, 2020, https://www.nejm.org/doi
    /full/10.1056/NEJMe2029812.

2. Editors, "Scientific American Endorses Joe Biden," *Scientific
    American*, October 1, 2020, https://www.scientificamerican.com
    /article/scientific-american-endorses-joe-biden1/.

3. David E. Sanger et al., "Before Virus Outbreak, a Cascade of
    Warnings Went Unheeded," *New York Times*, March 19, 2020,
    https://www.nytimes.com/2020/03/19/us/politics/trump
    -coronavirus-outbreak.html; Dan Riechmann, "Trump Disbanded
    NSC Pandemic Unit that Experts Had Praised," ABC News,
    March 14, 2020, https://abcnews.go.com/Politics/wireStory
    /trump-disbanded-nsc-pandemic-unit-experts-praised-69594177.

4. "US Says [It] Will Not Take Part in WHO Global Drugs,
    Vaccine Initiative Launch," Reuters, April 24, 2020, https://www
    .reuters.com/article/us-health-coronavirus-who-usa/us-says-will
    -not-take-part-in-who-global-drugs-vaccine-initiative-launch
    -idUSKCN2261WJ.

5. Nathan Rott, "World Leaders Address Collapse of the Natural
    World at the UN Biodiversity Summit," NPR, September 30,
    2020, https://www.npr.org/2020/09/30/918846788/world
    -leaders-address-collapse-of-the-natural-world-at-the-u-n
    -biodiversity-summ. The United States, Brazil, and Australia were

alone in not signing the summit's pledge to protect biodiversity. See also Luke Denne, "World Leaders Pledge to Protect Nature, But the US, Brazil and Australia Aren't Among Them," NBC News, October 16, 2020, https://www.nbcnews.com/news /world/world-leaders-pledge-protect-nature-u-s-brazil-australia -aren-n1243551.

6. Joseph Guzman, "In Newly Released Tape, Trump Says COVID-19 Is 'A Killer' that 'Rips You Apart,'" The Hill, September 15, 2020, https://thehill.com/changing-america /resilience/natural-disasters/516502-in-newly-released-tape -trump-says-covid-19-is-a.

7. Hillel Italie, "Woodward Defends Decision to Withhold Trump's Virus Comments," Associated Press, September 9, 2020, https://apnews.com/article/entertainment-donald-trump-bob -woodward-michael-pence-virus-outbreak -99916044401d8f8e24eb7bedfec1d5d2.

8. Dean Baker, *Rigged: How Globalization and the Rules of the Modern Economy Were Structured to Make the Rich Richer* (Washington, DC: Center for Economic and Policy Research, 2016). Available online at https://deanbaker.net/books/rigged.htm.

9. Martin Wolf, "The World Falls Apart as the US Withdraws," *Financial Times*, July 7, 2020, https://www.ft.com/content /7309b1bd-9d91-4eb5-a75c-a29d191367de.

10. Edward Wong, "The Rapture and the Real World: Mike Pompeo Blends Beliefs and Policy," *New York Times*, March 30, 2019, https://www.nytimes.com/2019/03/30/us/politics/pompeo -christian-policy.html.

11. Richard Hofstadter, *Anti-Intellectualism in American Life* (New York: Vintage, 1966) and *The Paranoid Style in American Politics* (New York: Vintage, 2008).

12. Robert Kagan, "A Superpower, Like It or Not," *Foreign Affairs*, March/April 2021, https://www.foreignaffairs.com/articles /united-states/2021-02-16/superpower-it-or-not.

13. Edward W. Said, "Embattled Landscapes, Unresolved Geographies" (Second Annual Eqbal Ahmad Lecture, Hampshire College, Amherst, MA, September 17, 1999).

14. John Nagl and Paul Yingling, "'. . . All Enemies, Foreign and Domestic': An Open Letter to Gen. Milley," *Defense One*, August 11, 2020, https://www.defenseone.com/ideas/2020/08/all-enemies -foreign-and-domestic-open-letter-gen-milley/167625/.

15. Barton Gellman, "The Election That Could Break America," *Atlantic*, September 23, 2020, https://www.theatlantic.com /magazine/archive/2020/11/what-if-trump-refuses-concede /616424/. See also Barton Gellman, "How Trump Could Attempt a Coup," *Atlantic*, November 2, 2020, https://www .theatlantic.com/politics/archive/2020/11/how-trump -could-attempt-coup/616954/.

16. Editors, "Dying in a Leadership Vacuum."

17. Noam Chomsky, *Deterring Democracy* (New York: Hill & Wang, 1992).

18. Paul Krugman, "Trump Is Killing the Economy Out of Spite," *New York Times*, October 9, 2020, A26.

19. Noam Chomsky and Robert Pollin, with C. J. Polychroniou, *Climate Crisis and the Global Green New Deal* (New York: Verso Books, 2020), 150.

20. Stanley Reed, "Chevron's Purchase Could Unlock Israel's Natural Gas Bonanza," *New York Times*, October 9, 2020, https://www .nytimes.com/2020/10/09/business/eastern-mediterranean-natural -gas-chevron.html.

21. Noam Chomsky and Marv Waterstone, *Consequences of Capitalism: Manufacturing Discontent and Resistance* (Chicago: Haymarket Books, 2021).

5. Class Struggle or Get It in the Neck

1. Rachel Martin and Lulu Garcia-Navarro, "News Brief: Coronavirus Pandemic, Biden Transition, Census Court Case," National Public Radio, *Morning Edition*, November 30, 2021, https://www.npr.org/2020/11/30/940037910/morning-news-brief.

2. Manny Fernandez et al., "As Surge Spreads, No Corner of Nation Is Spared," *New York Times*, November 26, 2020, A1.

3.   Frank Bruni, "Death Came for the Dakotas," *New York Times*, December 5, 2020, https://www.nytimes.com/2020/12/05/opinion /sunday/covid-north-south-dakota.html.

4.   Abigail Williams, "US Opts Out of WHO-Linked Global COVID-19 Vaccine Effort," NBC News, September 3, 2020, https://www.nbcnews.com/politics/white-house/u-s-opts-out -who-linked-global-covid-19-vaccine-n1239218.

5.   Patricia Zengerle and Steve Holland, "Trump's Vaccine Team Will Not Brief Biden Administration: U.S. Senators," Reuters, November 19, 2020, https://www.reuters.com/article/us-usa -election-vaccine/trumps-vaccine-team-will-not-brief-biden -administration-u-s-senators-idUSKBN27Z2UA.

6.   Quinnipiac University Poll, December 10, 2020, https://poll .qu.edu/Poll-Release?releaseid=3734.

7.   Donald Trump and Joe Biden, transcript of presidential debate, Nashville, Tennessee, October 22, 2020, CNN, https:// transcripts.cnn.com/show/se/date/2020-10-22/segment/02.

8.   Anthony DiMaggio, "Election 2020: A Democratic Mandate or a Vote Against Trump?" CounterPunch, November 24, 2020, https://www.counterpunch.org/2020/11/24/election -2020-a-democratic-mandate-or-a-vote-against-trump/.

9.   Howard Zinn, "Don't Despair about the Supreme Court," *Progressive*, October 21, 2005, https://progressive.org/op-eds /howard-zinn-despair-supreme-court/.

10.   Michael J. Klarman, *The Framers' Coup: The Making of the United States Constitution* (New York: Oxford University Press, 2016).

11.   Michael Crowley, Falih Hassan, and Eric Schmitt, "US Strike in Iraq Kills Qassim Suleimani, Commander of Iranian Forces," *New York Times*, January 2, 2020, https://www.nytimes.com/2020 /01/02/world/middleeast/qassem-soleimani-iraq-iran-attack.html; David E. Sanger et al., "Gunmen Assassinate Iran's Top Nuclear Scientist in Ambush, Provoking New Crisis," *New York Times*, November 27, 2020, https://www.nytimes.com/2020/11/28 /world/middleeast/iran-mohsen-fakhrizadeh-nuclear.html.

12.   David E. Sanger, "Assassination in Iran Could Limit Biden's Options. Was That the Goal?" *New York Times*, November 28,

2020, https://www.nytimes.com/2020/11/28/world/middleeast
/israel-iran-nuclear-deal.html.

13. Richard Pérez-Peña, Lara Jakes, and Farnaz Fassihi, "U.S. Calls
for Indefinite Arms Embargo of Iran, but Finds No Takers,"
New York Times, June 30, 2020, https://www.nytimes.com
/2020/06/30/world/middleeast/Iran-arms embargo.html.

14. Lara Jakes and David E. Sanger, "U.S. Reimposes UN Sanctions
on Iran Over Objections of World Powers," *New York Times*,
September 30, 2020, https://www.nytimes.com/2020/09/19/us
/politics/us-iran-un-sanctions.html.

15. Sanger, "Assassination in Iran."

16. Tony Barber, "Robert Fisk, Foreign Correspondent and Author,
1946–2020," *Financial Times*, November 6, 2020, https://www
.ft.com/content/349fe7bc-f889-46e8-980b-93d9a736aebc.

17. Jonathan Cook, "Establishment Journalists Are Piling On to
Smear Robert Fisk Now He Cannot Answer Back," *Jonathan
Cook Blog*, November 30, 2020, https://www.jonathan-cook.net
/blog/2020-11-30/journalists-smear-robert-fisk/.

18. Natalie Wolchover, "What Is a Particle?" *Quanta Magazine*,
November 12, 2020, https://www.quantamagazine.org/what-is-a
-particle-20201112/.

19. Mahmoud Darwish, "Under Siege," trans. Marjolijn De Jager,
Palestine-Israel Journal of Politics, Economics, and Culture 22, no.
2/3 (2017): 175.

6. Consequences of Capitalism

1. Noam Chomsky and Marv Waterstone, *Consequences of
Capitalism: Manufacturing Discontent and Resistance* (Chicago:
Haymarket Books, 2021), xiii.

2. David Hume, "Of the First Principles of Government," in *Hume:
Political Essays*, ed. Knud Haakonssen (Cambridge: Cambridge
University Press, 1994), 16.

3. Adam Smith, *The Wealth of Nations, Books I–III* (London:
Penguin Classics, 2000), Book III, ch. 4, 252.

4. Adam Smith, *The Wealth of Nations, Books IV–V* (London:
Penguin Classics, 2000), Book IV, chap. 1, 25.

5. Letter from James Madison to Thomas Jefferson, August 8, 1791, https://founders.archives.gov/documents/Madison /01-14-02-0062.

6. See Noam Chomsky, "Scholarship and Ideology: American Historians as 'Experts in Legitimation,'" *Social Scientist* 1, no. 7 (1973): 20–37, and *The Responsibility of Intellectuals*, 50th anniversary edition (New York: The New Press, 2017).

7. See Noam Chomsky, *Necessary Illusions: Thought Control in Democratic Societies* (Toronto: House of Anansi, 1995) and "The Divine License to Kill," in *Masters of Mankind: Essays and Lectures, 1969–2013* (Chicago: Haymarket Books, 2014), 57–73.

8. Walter Lippmann, *The Phantom Public: A Sequel to "Public Opinion"* (New York: Macmillan, 1927), 155.

9. Ralph Waldo Emerson, "Voluntaries," *Atlantic Monthly*, October 1863, https://www.theatlantic.com/magazine/archive/2012/02 /voluntaries/308825/.

10. Peter Carlson, "Nathaniel Hawthorne Disses Abe Lincoln," *American History*, October 2011, https://www.historynet.com /nathaniel-hawthorne-disses-abe-lincoln.htm.

11. Nathaniel Hawthorne, "Chiefly About War Matters, By a Peaceable Man," *Atlantic Monthly*, July 1862, https://www .theatlantic.com/magazine/archive/1862/07/chiefly-about -war-matters/306159/.

12. Mike Baker, "Seattle's Virus Success Shows What Could Have Been," *New York Times*, March 11, 2021, https://www.nytimes.com /2021/03/11/us/coronavirus-seattle-success.html.

13. Lindsay Wise, "McConnell Says '100%' of His Focus Is on Blocking Biden Agenda," *Wall Street Journal*, May 5, 2021, https://www.wsj.com/articles/mcconnell-says-100-of-his-focus -is-on-blocking-biden-agenda-11620257305.

14. Maggie Astor and Shane Goldmacher, "At Lewis Funeral, Obama Calls Filibuster a 'Jim Crow Relic,'" *New York Times*, July 30, 2020, https://www.nytimes.com/2020/07/30/us/politics /john-lewis-funeral-barack-obama.html.

15. Doyle Rice, "A Massive Iceberg—Larger than New York City— Breaks off Antarctica," *USA Today*, March 1, 2021, https://www

.usatoday.com/story/news/world/2021/03/01/massive-iceberg
-breaks-off-antarctica-brunt-ice-shelf/6869602002/.

16. See Noam Chomsky, *Turning the Tide: U.S. Intervention in Central America and the Struggle for Peace* (Chicago: Haymarket Books, 2014).

17. See Dana Frank, *The Long Honduran Night: Resistance, Terror, and the United States in the Aftermath of the Coup* (Chicago: Haymarket Books, 2018).

18. Emily Dixon, "Alexandria Ocasio-Cortez Was Asked About Defunding the Police and Her Answer Went Viral," *Marie Claire*, June 12, 2020, https://www.marieclaire.com/politics /a32849383/alexandria-ocasio-cortez-defund-the-police/.

19. Chomsky and Waterstone, *Consequences of Capitalism*, 91.

7. The United States Rules the World

1. Rajan Menon, "The Pandemic Is Us (But Now Mostly Them): Power, Wealth, and Justice in the Time of Covid-19," TomDispatch, June 20, 2021, https://tomdispatch.com/the -pandemic-is-us-but-now-mostly-them/.

2. Kylie Atwood, Kaitlan Collins, and Betsy Klein, "Biden Administration Finalizing Plans to Send Millions of AstraZeneca Vaccine Doses to Canada and Mexico," CNN, March 18, 2021, https://www.cnn.com/2021/03/17/politics /us-astrazeneca-mexico-canada/index.html.

3. Jack London, "The Unparalleled Invasion," *McClure's*, July 1910.

4. Stockholm International Peace Research Institute, "World Military Spending Rises to Almost $2 Trillion in 2020," April 26, 2021, https://www.sipri.org/media/press-release/2021/world -military-spending-rises-almost-2-trillion-2020.

5. Amnesty International, "Up to One Million Detained in China's 'Mass Re-education' Drive," September 2018, https://www .amnesty.org/en/latest/news/2018/09/china-up-to-one -million-detained/.

6. Edward S. Herman and Noam Chomsky, *Manufacturing Consent: The Political Economy of the Mass Media* (New York: Knopf, 2002), 37.

7. United Nations Human Development Reports, "Latest Human Development Index Ranking," 2020, http://hdr.undp.org/en /content/latest-human-development-index-ranking.

8. Amartya Sen, "Indian Development: Lessons and Non-Lessons," *Daedalus* 118, no. 4 (Fall 1989): 369–92. See also Amartya Sen, "More Than 100 Million Women Are Missing," *New York Review of Books*, December 20, 1990, https://www.nybooks.com/articles /1990/12/20/more-than-100-million-women-are-missing/.

9. Sen, "Indian Development."

10. Jean Drèze and Amartya Sen, *India: Economic Development and Social Opportunity* (New York: Oxford University Press, 1999).

11. Stéphane Courtois et al., *The Black Book of Communism: Crimes, Terror, Repression* (Cambridge, MA: Harvard University Press, 1999).

12. Andrew Chatzky and James McBride, "China's Massive Belt and Road Initiative," Council on Foreign Relations backgrounder, January 28, 2020, https://www.cfr.org/backgrounder/chinas -massive-belt-and-road-initiative.

13. Jeff Abbott, "United States Attacks Cuban Medics During Pandemic," *Progressive*, October 30, 2020, https://progressive.org /latest/us-attacks-cuban-medics-during-pandemic-abbott-201030/.

14. Ross Douthat, "The Strange Death of Liberal Russophobia," *New York Times*, June 19, 2021, https://www.nytimes.com/2021 /06/19/opinion/sunday/biden-putin-trump.html.

15. Dwight D. Eisenhower, "Chance for Peace" (speech addressed to the American Society of Newspaper Editors, Washington DC, April 16, 1953).

16. Editorial Board, "One Way Forward on Iran: A Nuclear-Weapons-Free Persian Gulf," *New York Times*, June 12, 2021, https://www.nytimes.com/2021/06/12/opinion/sunday/iran -nuclear-deal.html.

17. Alicia Sanders-Zakre, interviewed by Amy Goodman and Nermeen Shaikh, "US Led 2020 Nuclear Weapons Spending; Now Biden Going 'Full Steam Ahead' on Trump's Nuclear Plans," *Democracy Now!*, June 10, 2021, https://www .democracynow.org/2021/6/10/biden_putin_nuclear_weapons.

18. United Nations Office for Disarmament Affairs, "Treaty on the Prohibition of Nuclear Weapons," https://www.un.org /disarmament/wmd/nuclear/tpnw/.

19. Arundhati Roy, *Azadi: Freedom. Fascism. Fiction.* (Chicago: Haymarket Books, 2020).

20. Sanjay Kak, ed., *Witness: Kashmir 1986–2016/ Nine Photographers* (New Delhi: Yaarbal, 2017).

21. Jammu Kashmir Coalition of Civil Society, "Kashmir's Digital Siege," August 2020, https://jkccs.net/report-kashmirs -internet-siege/.

22. Gary Younge, "Archbishop Desmond Tutu: The Secrets of a Peacemaker," *Guardian*, May 22, 2009, https://www.theguardian .com/books/2009/may/23/interview-desmond-tutu.

23. Howard Zinn, *A People's History of the United States* (New York: Harper Perennial Modern Classics), 688.

8. Tipping Points: Environmental and Political

1. Lynsey Chutel, "Most African Countries Missed a Target to Vaccinate 10 Percent of Their People," *New York Times*, September 30, 2021, https://www.nytimes.com/2021/09/30 /world/africa/africa-covid-vaccine.html.

2. David Leonhardt, "Red America's Covid Problem," *New York Times*, June 28, 2021, https://www.nytimes.com/2021/06/28 /briefing/covid-cases-rising-red-america.html.

3. Martin Wolf, "The Strange Death of American Democracy," *Financial Times*, September 28, 2021, https://www.ft.com/content /a2e499d0-10f0-4fa2-8243-e23eedc4f9f4.

4. Intergovernmental Panel on Climate Change, "Climate Change Widespread, Rapid, and Intensifying–IPCC," August 9, 2021, https://www.ipcc.ch/2021/08/09/ar6-wg1-20210809-pr/.

5. Trevor Hunnicutt and Jeff Mason, "US Calls on OPEC and its Allies to Pump More Oil," Reuters, August 11, 2021, https:// www.reuters.com/world/middle-east/us-call-opec-its-allies -increase-oil-production-cnbc-2021-08-11/.

6. António Guterres, "Secretary-General Calls Latest IPCC Climate Report 'Code Red for Humanity,' Stressing 'Irrefutable' Evidence

of Human Influence," August 9, 2021, https://www.un.org
/press/en/2021/sgsm20847.doc.htm.

7. Recognizing the Duty of the Federal Government to Create a
Green New Deal, H.R. 109, 116th Congress (2019–2020).

8. Rana Foroohar, "Place Matters," *Financial Times*, November 16,
2020, https://www.ft.com/content/9321de36-92ae-46ea-8bf1
-24597808af68.

9. N. Gregory Mankiw, "Can America Afford to Become a Major
Social Welfare State?" *New York Times*, September 15, 2021,
https://www.nytimes.com/2021/09/15/opinion/biden-spending
-plan-welfare.html.

10. António Guterres, "Launching 'United in Science' Climate
Report, Secretary-General Stresses Need to Prevent Further
Irreversible Damage, Warning 'We Are Out of Time,'"
September 16, 2021, https://www.un.org/press/en/2021
/sgsm20905.doc.htm.

11. United Mine Workers, "Preserving Coal Country: Keeping
America's Coal Miners, Families and Communities Whole in an
Era of Global Energy Transition," April 2021, https://umwa
.org/wp-content/uploads/2021/04/UMWA-Preserving-Coal
-Country-2021.pdf.

12. Arlie Russell Hochschild, *Strangers in Their Own Land: Anger and
Mourning on the American Right* (New York: The New Press, 2018).

13. Edward W. Said, *Orientalism* (New York: Vintage, 2003), xxi.

14. John Stuart Mill, "A Few Words on Non-Intervention" (1859),
republished in *New England Review* 27, no. 3 (2006): 252–64.

15. Noam Chomsky and Ilan Pappé, *Gaza in Crisis: Reflections on
Israel's War Against the Palestinians*, ed. Frank Barat (Chicago:
Haymarket Books, 2010), 79–124. See also Joseph Conrad,
Heart of Darkness and Selections from The Congo Diary, ed. Carryl
Churchill (New York: Modern Library, 1999), xlii.

16. Quoted in William Earl Weeks, *John Quincy Adams and American
Global Empire* (Lexington, KY: University Press of Kentucky,
2002), 193.

17. Tariq Ali, "Afghanistan, China and the Decline of US Power,"
Alternative Radio, September 9, 2021.

18. Anatol Lieven, "On the Road: Interview with Commander Abdul Haq," October 14, 2001, https://carnegieendowment.org /2001/10/14/on-road-interview-with-commander-abdul-haq -pub-818. Lieven interviewed Abdul Haq in Peshawar on October 11, 2001.

19. "Pentagon Briefing with Secretary Rumsfeld," *Washington Post*, November 19, 2001, https://www.washingtonpost.com/wp-srv /nation/specials/attacked/transcripts/rumsfeldtext_111901.html.

20. Editor's note: David Barsamian has been banned from entering India since 2011 because of his journalism.

21. Noam Chomsky and Robert Pollin, with C. J. Polychroniou, *Climate Crisis and the Global Green New Deal* (New York: Verso Books, 2020), 148.

22. Noam Chomsky, "The Future of American Power," *Economist*, September 24, 2021, https://www.economist.com/by-invitation /2021/09/24/noam-chomsky-on-the-cruelty-of-american -imperialism.

9. Optimism of the Will

1. International Institute for Democracy and Electoral Assistance, "Global State of Democracy Report 2021: Building Resilience in a Pandemic Era," 2021, https://www.idea.int/gsod/global-report.

2. Barton Gellman, "The Election That Could Break America," *Atlantic*, September 23, 2020, https://www.theatlantic.com /magazine/archive/2020/11/what-if-trump-refuses-concede/616424/.

3. Nick Hanauer and David M. Rolf, "The Top 1% of Americans Have Taken $50 Trillion From the Bottom 90%—And That's Made the US Less Secure," *Time*, September 14, 2020, https:// time.com/5888024/50-trillion-income-inequality-america/.

4. Gordon Lafer, "The Legislative Attack on American Wages and Labor Standards, 2011–2012," Economic Policy Institute, October 31, 2013, https://www.epi.org/publication/attack -on-american-labor-standards/.

5. Ursula K. Le Guin, "Speech in Acceptance of the National Book Foundation Medal for Distinguished Contribution to American

Letters," November 19, 2014, https://www.ursulakleguin.com
/nbf-medal.

6. Noam Chomsky, *Masters of Mankind: Essays and Lectures,*
1969–2013 (Chicago: Haymarket Books, 2014), 139–46.

7. Chomsky, *Masters of Mankind,* 141–42.

8. David E. Sanger, Steven Erlanger, and Roger Cohen, "Biden Tells
Allies 'America Is Back,' but Macron and Merkel Push Back,"
New York Times, February 19, 2021, https://www.nytimes.com
/2021/02/19/us/politics/biden-munich-conference.html.

9. Tucker Carlson, "Tucker Carlson: America Would Gain Nothing
from Starting War with Russia," Fox News, December 8, 2021,
https://www.foxnews.com/opinion/tucker-carlson-america
-gain-nothing-from-starting-war-russia.

10. Noam Chomsky, interviewed by Junaid Ahmad, "Noam Chomsky
on 'The China Threat,'" Daanish TV English (Pakistan), November
10, 2021, https://ne-np.facebook.com/DaanishTV/videos/noam
-chomsky-the-taliban-have-a-solid-base-in-the-community
-daanish-tv-english/3005024773085270/.

11. Piero Gleijeses, *Conflicting Missions: Havana, Washington,*
and Africa, 1959–1976 (Chapel Hill, NC: University of North
Carolina Press, 2003), 26

12. John Quincy Adams, *Writings of John Quincy Adams,* ed.
Worthington Chauncey Ford, vol. 7 (New York: Macmillan,
1917), 373.

13. United Nations News, "UN General Assembly Calls for US to
End Cuba Embargo for 29th Consecutive Year," June 23, 2021,
https://news.un.org/en/story/2021/06/1094612.

14. Paul Keating, "Morrison Is Making an Enemy of China—and
Labor Is Helping Him," *Sydney Morning Herald,* September 22,
2021, https://www.smh.com.au/world/asia
/morrison-is-making-an-enemy-of-china-and-labor-is-helping-
him-20210921-p58tek.html.

15. Antonio Gramsci, *Prison Notebooks,* ed. and trans. by Joseph A.
Buttigieg with Antonio Callari, 3 vols (New York: Columbia
University Press, 2011).

INDEX

225

ABOUT HAYMARKET BOOKS

Haymarket Books is a radical, independent, nonprofit book publisher based in Chicago. Our mission is to publish books that contribute to struggles for social and economic justice. We strive to make our books a vibrant and organic part of social movements and the education and development of a critical, engaged, international left.

We take inspiration and courage from our namesakes, the Haymarket martyrs, who gave their lives fighting for a better world. Their 1886 struggle for the eight-hour day—which gave us May Day, the international workers' holiday—reminds workers around the world that ordinary people can organize and struggle for their own liberation. These struggles continue today across the globe—struggles against oppression, exploitation, poverty, and war.

Since our founding in 2001, Haymarket Books has published more than five hundred titles. Radically independent, we seek to drive a wedge into the risk-averse world of corporate book publishing. Our authors include Noam Chomsky, Arundhati Roy, Rebecca Solnit, Angela Y. Davis, Howard Zinn, Amy Goodman, Wallace Shawn, Mike Davis, Winona LaDuke, Ilan Pappé, Richard Wolff, Dave Zirin, Keeanga-Yamahtta Taylor, Nick Turse, Dahr Jamail, David Barsamian, Elizabeth Laird, Amira Hass, Mark Steel, Avi Lewis, Naomi Klein, and Neil Davidson. We are also the trade publishers of the acclaimed Historical Materialism Book Series and of Dispatch Books.

ALSO AVAILABLE FROM HAYMARKET BOOKS

Chronicles of Dissent
Interviews with David Barsamian, 1984–1996
David Barsamian and Noam Chomsky

Confronting Empire
Eqbal Ahmad and David Barsamian
Foreword by Pervez Hoodbhoy and Edward W. Said

Consequences of Capitalism: Manufacturing Discontent and Resistance
Noam Chomsky and Marv Waterstone

Culture and Resistance
David Barsamian and Edward W. Said

Gaza in Crisis
Reflections on the US–Israeli War Against the Palestinians
Noam Chomsky and Ilan Pappé

Hopes and Prospects
Noam Chomsky

Optimism over Despair
On Capitalism, Empire, and Social Change
Noam Chomsky and C.J. Polychroniou

On Palestine
Noam Chomsky and Ilan Pappé, edited by Frank Barat

Masters of Mankind: Essays and Lectures, 1969–2013
Noam Chomsky, foreword by Marcus Raskin